What people are saying about …

HOPE UNLEASHED

"Andy packs his usual pace, energy, and enthusiasm into this fantastic book, urging us to give absolutely everything we've got to preaching the gospel. The result is both challenging and inspirational as it unpacks the biblical basis for word and action mission, tackles big issues head-on, and motivates us to keep going when things get tough. For anyone serious about following God's call, don't just read this book—really take it to heart and live it out."

Mike Pilavachi, founder of Soul Survivor

"This easy-to-read book has ingredients of faith-inspiring stories, biblical teachings and images, plus experienced mature observations from a pioneer of the gospel. It deserves to be read by every church member who wants to reach their area and networks with the gospel."

Gerald Coates, founder of Pioneer

"*Hope Unleashed* is not a theoretical book outlining God's plans for mission, but is practical, down to earth, and inspiring, full of nitty-gritty stories of God at work in the lives of ordinary people like you and me. It takes seriously God's love for people and shows how his love can be expressed through both words and actions."

Steve Clifford, general director
of Evangelical Alliance

"The new paradigm—that is not new at all but has a truth that has been lost—is word and action evangelism. Andy's passion and practical insights *could*(!) cause the transformation we all long for in our villages, towns, and cities. This is a timely, prophetic insight for the culture in which we find ourselves."

Roy Crowne, vice president of Youth for Christ

ANDY HAWTHORNE

HOPE
UNLEASHED

ANDY HAWTHORNE

HOPE UNLEASHED

SERVING GOD THROUGH WORDS AND ACTIONS

David C Cook®

transforming lives together

HOPE UNLEASHED
Published by David C. Cook
4050 Lee Vance View
Colorado Springs, CO 80918 U.S.A.

David C. Cook Distribution Canada
55 Woodslee Avenue, Paris, Ontario, Canada N3L 3E5

David C. Cook U.K., Kingsway Communications
Eastbourne, East Sussex BN23 6NT, England

Survivor is an imprint of David C. Cook
Kingsway Communications Ltd
info@survivor.co.uk

David C. Cook and the graphic circle C logo
are registered trademarks of Cook Communications Ministries.

The Web site addresses recommended throughout this book are offered as a
resource to you. These Web sites are not intended in any way to be or imply an
endorsement on the part of David C. Cook, nor do we vouch for their content.

All Scripture quotations are taken from the *Holy Bible,
New International Version*®. *NIV*®. Copyright © 1973, 1978, 1984 by
International Bible Society. Used by permission of Zondervan. All rights
reserved. The author has added italics to Scripture for emphasis.

Quote from *A Box of Delights* by J.John and Mark Stibbe
(© 2001) used by permission of Monarch Books.

LCCN 2009905010
ISBN 978-1-4347-6448-5
eISBN 978-0-7814-0338-2

© 2009 Andy Hawthorne

The Team: Les Moir, Richard Herkes, Sally Johnson, Amy Kiechlin,
Sarah Schultz, Jack Campbell, and Karen Athen
Cover Design: Mark Prentice

Printed in the United States of America
First Edition 2009

1 2 3 4 5 6 7 8 9 10

052709

TO BETH

This book is dedicated to you because you're amazing and because God really does have great plans for your life.

CONTENTS

Foreword 11

Acknowledgments 15

Introduction: Two Phone Calls 17

1. There Is No Plan B *(Luke 1:26–56)* 25

2. Not Fluffy Bunnies or Facebook *(Luke 4:16–19)* 41

3. Getting into the Boat *(Luke 4:29—5:11)* 55

4. A Question of Healing *(Luke 5:12–26)* 69

5. The Halftime Break *(Luke 7:36–50)* 81

6. I Never Liked the Floor That Much Anyway *(Luke 8:1–15)* 93

7. God Said Okay and Disappeared … *(Luke 8:26–39)* 105

8. Heaven Takes a Breath *(Luke 9:1–9; 10:1–24)* 121

9. More Than Just Leftovers *(Luke 9:10–17)* 135

10. Tribute Bands and Bread and Wine *(Luke 22:7–20)* 147

Closing Thoughts 161

Supporting The Message? 173

FOREWORD

There are seven qualities I love about this book.

1. Vision: Andy is a person of vision, and yet he is a team player with a wisdom and a balance that are evident throughout this book. Balance is so needed in God's work today. In my own walk with Jesus, now over fifty-four years, I have seen too many people fall into the trap of extremism and unbalance. This message will help people avoid that pitfall.

2. Faith: None of us can walk with God and do his will if we do not exercise faith. The Eden Project story and so many other aspects of ministry that we read about in these pages will help us take steps of faith in our own lives and ministries. It is so easy to just be singers and hearers of the Word and not so much to be doers! I pray this book will help break the barrier and thrust many people into the action.

3. *Grace* is such an important word and concept, in my opinion, and I love the way it comes out in this book. Andy doesn't tie us up in duty but shows how Jesus inspires a life of gratitude and service.

4. Community: This has become a key concept in recent years. Andy wants to see transformed lives that will really bless

and influence the community. We are not talking about Utopia or perfection, but we are talking about reality. Here is a model we can follow, as we contextualize it to our own pilgrimage and experience.

5. Prayer: I so appreciate the emphasis on prayer. We do not hear or see enough of that in this context. The picture of people involved in prayer should cause others to want to get involved with praying people and gather where prayer is a reality.

6. Urgency: I believe this is often a missed reality in the lives of many of the Lord's servants and leads to a massive waste of time with little realization that we are surrounded by lost people who need the Savior. The clear challenge for all of us to share our faith is a vital part of the message of this book. The way God can change lives and use ordinary people should push all of us into action and into a life of redeeming the time to reach more people with the message.

7. *Proactive* is one of my favorite words, and it describes Andy and his team and The Message Trust in general. By faith, love, and action they have made things happen, and many are being transformed and on the way to heaven because of it. This work has gone on for many years and is a proven ministry that is here to stay. At the same time, they need our prayers and support, and we need to ask God to show us what he would have us do about this great message, great vision, and great ministry.

I want to urge you to take time to read this book and other similar books. The neglect of reading serious books written by men and women of God is a huge hindrance to what our God wants to do in the world today. No wonder we are not seeing many long-term missionaries heading out to the more forgotten and unreached places of the world! Let's get a few extra copies of this message and pass it on to others.

George Verwer
Founder of Operation Mobilisation

ACKNOWLEDGMENTS

Thanks to Craig for all the input and inspiration and for making my work so much better.

To everyone at Survivor and to all the wonderful Message supporters, staff, trustees, and volunteers—what a team!

Finally, thank you, God; I'd be in deep trouble without you, and I want the world to know how amazing you are.

.

INTRODUCTION

TWO PHONE CALLS

I've just had a couple of phone calls that are making me think. Nothing much unusual about that—the phone calls or the thinking. But still, I can't quite shift the feeling that what I've just heard is in some way significant.

For over twenty years I've been leading The Message Trust. We're based in Manchester, England, where we live, breathe, eat, and sleep our single vision: to see the place where we live blitzed, bombed, and overpowered by the good news expressed through words and actions. At the very heart of things you'll find us stirred up about going into the toughest places and reaching the most forgotten people. I'm not on the front lines as much as I used to be, but I keep in touch as best I can. And that's why I've had these two conversations within the last few hours.

The first one was from an excited Lindsay West. That's not a technical term for bad weather; he's the guy who fronts our band LZ7. He was calling to tell me about his week. He's been in a school since Monday and the week's just peaked with a big evangelistic gig to which all the pupils were invited. Like I said, he was pretty excited, but somehow through the repetitions of words like "awesome," "amazing," and, for some reason, "gangsta, mate," I worked it out: He'd had a very good week. God had shown up, and 160 young people had just committed their lives to Christ.

The next call was from the guy who heads up our mission department, Matt Wilson. He was asking me to pray for two of our courageous Eden workers. They've made the choice to live long-term on one of Manchester's toughest estates, an area the locals used to call "The Bronx." These two girls on our team have given their lives to serving and blessing that community, to living their faith out loud among people the rest of society would rather ignore. The results have been amazing: The church has grown, crime has come down, and the whole community has received a much-needed dose of the kindness of God. But Matt was calling to tell me that our girls had just had their car set on fire by one of their more unbalanced neighbors. The car was a write-off, and the front window of their house had been blown out in the blast.

These two phone calls have got me thinking: Why does it always seem to be like this? The more we push out and see good things happening, the more opposition we run into. Yet again I find myself wondering what our priorities should be. Should we be trying for the "lamp on a stand" approach—bold, unashamed gospel proclamation to thousands of school kids? Or should we be pushing more toward "salt" and "yeast"—serving and blessing the vulnerable and the marginalized with no questions asked?

Both. That's the only answer that makes sense. And of course that can't be true just for us in The Message Trust—it's for every real Christian who has decided to follow Jesus. We must do both.

In this book we are going to look at how we can find that balance. We'll be looking at what works, as well as wondering about what doesn't. And all along we'll be learning from the Master. We'll start by jumping into Luke's gospel. I love the fact that Jesus' whole life's work is based on what we read in Luke 4. There he is, just out of the desert, in the power of the Spirit, entering the synagogue. By one of those God-directed coincidences it "just so happens" to be his turn to read the Scriptures, and the set reading for the day "just so happens" to be Isaiah 61:

> The Spirit of the Lord is on me, because he has
> anointed me to preach good news to the poor.
> He has sent me to proclaim freedom for the
> prisoners and recovery of sight for the blind,
> to release the oppressed, to proclaim the year
> of the Lord's favor. (Luke 4:18–19)

This is Jesus talking. This is Jesus reaching back into history, rooted in the present and looking forward into the future, holding all things in balance as he goes on to preach one of the shortest but best sermons ever: "Today this scripture is fulfilled in your hearing" (verse 21). That was it, just eight words. And for the next three and a half years it was precisely what Jesus did. He fulfilled the prophecy by preaching good news, setting captives free, and opening the eyes of the blind wherever he went.

And he's still doing it today.

There's a problem though. Almost from the very moment that Jesus spoke those eight words, people around him have been spending inordinate amounts of time trying to decide what life's priorities ought to be. We're still wondering about it today. The word-only guys argue that our primary aim must be the preaching of the good news. The power-evangelism guys are more likely to emphasize the miraculous healing of the blind. And the liberation theologians say that what really counts is releasing the captives.

But hold on a moment: Surely our role model did it all, in perfect harmony. What's more, when Jesus introduced us to the Holy Spirit, he used the words "As the Father has sent me, I am sending you" (John 20:21). So, perhaps he really *did* expect us, wherever possible, to explain the good news with our words while also ensuring that we demonstrate the gospel with our actions.

Ever since I was a baby Christian, I've grown up on a solid diet of Bible teaching. My background is full of words, and I was taught to favor them over action anytime. It's hardly surprising that I became an evangelist and that I love to preach. I remember a wealthy businessman in our church saying to me years ago that he couldn't give his money to a Christian relief and development charity because they didn't make preaching the gospel a priority. What he meant was, they didn't necessarily use words to preach the gospel; and to him, therefore, they weren't quite coming up to scratch. Sure, they were feeding people and helping them live a little longer, but that seemed less important than actually telling the people about Jesus and getting them to convert. "Preach the gospel in season and out of season" was the mantra I had grown up with. As far as I could tell, there was no excuse to stop blabbing about Jesus.

So it came as a bit of a shock to me when around ten years ago, in the buildup to a huge citywide outreach we were planning, one of our partners sat me down and told me he was convinced that at least half the young people involved should be out there performing random acts of kindness. I was surprised. What on earth did washing someone's car have to do with the gospel? How did painting park benches lead to salvation? I didn't remember Jesus talking about the importance of weeding communal gardens. Still, I gave in, and our team started organizing around four hundred community action projects across the region.

Nearly decade has passed, and I can now say without a shadow of a doubt (and with only a little frustration!) that he was right and I was wrong. Jesus had loads to say about the way we live, and this model of mission—where our actions matter just as much as our words—has permanently shaped the way many of us do outreach.

There was something remarkable about that time we spent together in the summer of 2000. It was as if we did ten years' work in ten days. Perhaps some of our earlier attempts at "hit and run evangelism" had led people to believe that we were some kind of foaming-at-the-mouth fundamentalists. But suddenly we had the police and local authorities on our side, seeing us as a real force for good rather than a force to be avoided.

Since then we have learned a lot about "servant evangelism," as we've got involved in around a thousand more community action projects in every corner of Greater Manchester. We've cleaned and painted and fixed and helped, and as a result crime has come down, whole areas have been changed, and—yes—we've been privileged to have some great new opportunities to share our faith. A national movement of people fired up about doing mission in words and action has been birthed, and gradually, across Britain, the future for individuals, families, and whole communities is changing as a result.

There's no surprise that young people have really started to get busy in their own communities. Wherever you go, it doesn't take long before you run into someone who can quote those famous words of Francis of Assisi: "Preach the gospel at all times, and if necessary use words." There's just a slight problem with this: I don't really feel that these words from the great man describe the heart of what we do at all. To me, a much better way of describing this out-of-control God movement would be "preach the gospel at all times, using all the best words and actions you have."

There's plenty of truth in the saying that you can't get a ten-ton truck across a one-ton bridge, especially when you apply it to our attempts to preach. Too often we're heavy with the message but forget that our relationship with the community isn't anywhere near developed or strong enough to be able to cope with it. However, the flip side is also true: If we build a beautiful, highly polished bridge of kindness and yet never bring the truck of truth across, we haven't gotten the job done either. Some churches and youth groups are great at community action and social engagement; some are brilliant at gospel proclamation. For me the secret to success in any ministry is to genuinely combine the two.

I've become increasingly convinced of two things: First, God has given his church more than enough resources to ensure that every man, woman, and child hear the good news of Jesus in language they can understand. And second, every man, woman, and child can experience the kindness of our servant-hearted Savior through his people's actions. I'm praying that leaders around the world will rise to the challenge, follow his example, and take decisive steps to see the gospel demonstrated and hear it proclaimed in every corner of our planet.

In Acts 1:1, Luke starts his follow-up to his gospel. He writes,

> In my former book, Theophilus, I wrote about
> all that Jesus *began* to do and to teach.

Of course, his former book is the very gospel of Luke that we will be looking at across these pages. In one sense Luke's gospel *was* the story of everything Jesus did and said. But as we know, through the Holy Spirit, it is now *we* who are continuing Jesus' work. Look back at the first words of Acts and the word I highlighted—Jesus *began* the work. Through the power of the Holy Spirit, that work is still going on. How? Through people like you and me.

It's both daunting and exciting. One thing I am convinced of is that we must work hard to get the balance right. We have to discipline ourselves to ditch the dualism that says that it's only words that matter, or that actions win out every time. We have to have both. Why? Because that's how Jesus did it.

1

THERE IS NO PLAN B

Luke 1:26–56

Toward the end of a life full of amazing words and actions, Jesus said something that was remarkable even by his own standards. Talking to his Father, he said, "I have brought you glory on earth by completing the work you gave me to do" (John 17:4).

It strikes me that, like Jesus, we really do all have a task to complete on this earth and that the goal of our lives should be to get as close to completing that work as we possibly can. Flip the thought over: Isn't it absolutely amazing to think of all the good works we'll leave behind when we die? What about all those plans and possibilities that were dreamt up for us? Can we really ignore them so easily?

Jesus' good works here on earth didn't start when he came out of the desert in a blaze of glorious healing, teaching, and saving.

It was thirty years earlier that it all started, when he was willing to leave the glory of heaven and humble himself to float around as a fetus inside a little bag of waters in the womb of a young peasant girl. That's how far he had to go in order to get right alongside us, to reach our level and literally put flesh on the bones of God's master plan of salvation.

Throughout the rest of this book we will be looking at Jesus and seeing what we can learn from the way he reached out with words and actions. But first we need to go right back to the beginning and take a look at his mother. What can we learn from her amazing response to the call of God on her life?

There is no doubt that Mary was a remarkable young woman. How many girls in their early teens, as she probably was, would cope in such a faith-filled and chilled-out way in the face of such earth-shattering news? And it wasn't as if the delivery was low-key. There was no email, no gentle chat with a familiar family member; just some forty-foot-tall shining white angel called Gabriel. (Okay, so the Bible might not say he was forty feet tall or shining white, but you've got to give an evangelist a little room to tell a story!)

> The angel said to her, "Do not be afraid, Mary, you have found favor with God. You will be with child and give birth to a son, and you are to give him the name Jesus. He will be great and will be called the Son of the Most High. The Lord God will give him the throne of his

father David, and he will reign over the house
of Jacob forever; his kingdom will never end."
(Luke 1:30–33)

Let's be fair: Mary was a risk. What if she had said "No thanks"?
What if she got freaked out by the whole thing and changed her
mind? What if she ran off and drank a bottle of gin or had a cold
bath or found some other way of getting rid of the baby? There must
have been others looking for a way of dealing with an unexpected
pregnancy. What if Mary joined them?

The whole thing was a risk, and it's not much different today.
Imagine choosing you and me to share the most glorious news in
the world and to deliver the kindness of God to a hurting world!
What if we ran in the opposite direction? What if we gave up on
prayer, stopped acting in faith, and acted in fear instead? How
much of a mess the world would be in!

But that's our God. He has staked everything on us getting our
act together. He has bet the house on everyday idiots like you and
me getting involved and taking our faith seriously. How amazing
is that? How scary?

There is a folktale of the angels coming before God as Jesus
ascended to heaven. They were asking him what the plan was now
that Jesus' time on earth was up. Who was going to carry on the
work of building God's kingdom? God points down to the ragtag
bunch of anger-management failures, hotheads, and doubting
Thomases. It's them. They're the ones to build it.

"But what if they fail?"

"There is no plan B."

Those first disciples were the plan, just like that overwhelmed teenage mom, just like you and me. We're the plan. We're the potential. We're the way this thing gets built.

Mary may have been young, inexperienced, and poor, but she was no failure. She had what it took to be used by God; she had a heart that pumped for him, a heart that beat in time with his own work. As the eyes of the Lord scanned Israel looking for a girl who would be suitable for the greatest responsibility in the history of the world, they rested on Mary.

I love Mary's response to Gabriel's words. I'm convinced that if we were to respond in a similar way when each of us met our own calling, we would see a lot more success and transformation going on down here.

Four things stand out to me. First, there's the whole sense of urgency that we get from Mary. Luke 1:39 tells us that her response to the overwhelming responsibility was to get ready and hurry to Zechariah and Elizabeth's house to tell them the good news. Look at the rest of the gospels, and you'll see a whole lot of hurrying once people have received a word from the Lord. The gospels are littered with words like *immediately, suddenly,* and *swiftly.* Wouldn't it be great if the church of Jesus was a bit swifter to respond to the command of God to *go?* How much better would things be if we were to go out of our meetings with a little more pace and passion and deliver the good news in words and actions to this generation? For Mary there was no option. God had spoken, and she started to hurry.

That hurrying carried on over sixty miles of difficult terrain, but it was worth it. Once she arrived at Zechariah and Elizabeth's house, Elizabeth's baby started jumping for joy in the Holy Spirit. As if she needed it, there was Mary's massive confirmation that this wonderful miracle really was taking place inside her. In one quick trip Mary demonstrated a truth that lies at the heart of all Christian living: We have to understand the importance of sacrifice and obedience. If God puts people on your heart, don't just pray for them; go to them quickly and watch what he does. If God puts an neighborhood or a people group or a country in your mind, go quickly; don't wait until every piece of the jigsaw puzzle is in place and every penny is in the bank. Step out. Do it. Risk it.

After thirty years of doing this stuff, I can testify that if it's the Great Commission you're working on, God really will bankroll the work. Right now his eyes are searching the earth looking for people with a heart for the lost, hurting, or broken of this planet. And when he finds them and sees that they are ready to obey the call and go sacrificially, he will strongly support them (2 Chronicles 16:9).

The second thing that gets me is Mary's excitement. We've just had a few of our team return from a large youth prayer event in America called The Ramp, and to be honest I'm slightly worried they might spontaneously combust. They're so pumped that every talk we give is now greeted with whoops and hollers American style, and they're spending literally hours and hours of every day in prayer, worship, and sharing Jesus with people who don't know him. They're not doing it because they're paid or because they are bored or because they think it might just be a bit of a laugh. They're doing it because the reality of who Jesus is and what he did has burrowed deep under their skin. And when that happens for real, any aspect of our lives is a candidate for transformation.

I'm quite jealous of their passion right now. Granted, some of it may seem a bit over the top, but I'd rather have overenthusiasm than the numbness that comes from being lukewarm. George Verwer put it better when he said, "It's easier to cool down a furnace than warm up a corpse." I'd rather be a furnace for Jesus, and passion and excitement have always been the currency that young people deal in.

Luke carries on with the story:

> When Elizabeth heard Mary's greeting, the baby leaped in her womb, and Elizabeth was filled with the Holy Spirit. In a loud voice she exclaimed: "Blessed are you among women, and blessed is the child you will bear! But why am I so favored, that the mother of my Lord should come to me?" (Luke 1:41–43)

Elizabeth's joy was palpable. She was telling Mary that she was the most blessed person on the planet, that she had been given the most privileged job that's ever been given. Because Mary had not been tripped up or freaked out by the news, nor did she feel lukewarm about it—choosing instead to believe, trust, and act—Elizabeth could see that things were going well. There's a truth in here somewhere, that when we hold on tight to God's promises and believe that they will come through in spite of all the troubles and opposition around us, then we end up being blessed. So many Christians get disillusioned and discouraged when God's promises aren't fulfilled according to their schedules. It can be tempting to do the opposite of Mary and give in to disillusionment and defeat. But there is no life to be found down that route.

I think Mary knew that, because instinctively she joined in with Elizabeth's excitement, bursting into a song full with joy and optimism.

Mary said: "My soul glorifies the Lord and my spirit rejoices in God my Savior, for he has been mindful of the humble state of his servant. From now on all generations will call me blessed, for the Mighty One has done great things for me—holy is his name. His mercy extends to those who fear him, from generation to generation. He has performed mighty deeds with his arm; he has scattered those who are proud in their inmost thoughts. He has brought down rulers from their thrones but has lifted up the humble. He has filled the hungry with good things but has sent the rich away empty. He has helped his servant Israel,

remembering to be merciful to Abraham and
his descendants forever, even as he said to our
fathers." (Luke 1:46–55)

For most of my life I've been a member of my local Anglican church. Just occasionally I've had the joy of sitting through the 1662 prayer-book service. As the name suggests, this is a very old bit of kit. Over 350 years have passed since it was scripted by a bunch of evangelists called the Reformers. They were trying to reach people with the gospel, dragging services out of the world of outdated Latin traditions. They used the language of the street, and in its day it was a truly dangerous and radical thing to do. Their motto was "always reforming," and that's what they did, constantly bringing the services up to date, refusing to settle and be stuck in a rut. There was just one problem: One by one they were burnt at the stake for their efforts. Three and a half centuries later many churches are still using the same services. I've got a sneaking feeling that Thomas Cranmer and his fellow Reformers are in heaven right now slapping their heads, wincing their eyes shut, and shouting, *"Duh!"*

I know I'm on thin ice with some people, particularly those who love the poetry and reverence of the 1662 prayer-book service. And just because it's not my cup of tea doesn't mean God doesn't like it. But I'm sure that what matters more than whether we like the worship service or whether it's got robed choirs and bells and smells or screaming rock bands up front is whether the people outside the church can understand and connect with it. If that's not possible, we should do exactly what the Reformers did: Kick it out.

But I'll say this for the 1662 service: It nearly always includes Mary's song, called the Magnificat. This is an amazing collection of words held together by full-throttle joy, passion, and excitement. Sadly, in my experience, it usually gets sung to a miserable tune by people with very long faces, which is weird because this is a song of excitement and over-the-top joy and passion.

"My spirit rejoices in God my Savior...." The word *rejoices* here in the original Greek language is *agallio*. It's the same word that's used in Luke 10:21 when Jesus is freaking out with joy as the disciples return from their first mission and report that "even the demons submit to us in your name" (verse 17). It literally means "to leap for joy, to show one's joy by leaping and skipping, demonstrating excessive or ecstatic joy and delight." Mary is, in short, quite a happy girl at this point! In fact, it would appear that, despite the challenges of her pregnant state, she is beaming with excitement and almost bursting with this song of joy and praise to God.

Let's be fair, even with the hassle and hard work, Christianity is a phenomenally exciting thing. Living on the cutting edge of God's purposes, dealing with all the opposition that comes with trying to reach out into our communities, following Jesus' great commission to tell the world the good news … these are the ingredients that lead to the most real, most inspiring, most satisfying experience of all. Let's not lose the sheer joy and wonder of what this good news of Jesus can do in the darkest of communities and the most broken lives. Put another way, the gospel works every time; it's lost none of its power. As Paul says, we're plugged into "the power of God for the salvation of everyone who believes" (Romans 1:16). When you think about that, it's understandable that every once in a while—just like our young men returned from The Ramp—we need to get a little overexcited.

Right now the developed world is suffering from an epidemic of excess that is squeezing all the joy out of so many lives. Look around and you'll see it: an excess of alcohol, drugs, sex, debt, and isolation that is literally killing people. How about confronting that with the excessive, ecstatic joy and delight that only Jesus can bring?

The third thing that is obvious from Mary's response to God's call is her love of Scripture. She is thirteen or fourteen years old, yet she just oozes the Bible. This song she bursts into certainly feels as though it's off the top of her head, but it includes no less than twelve different Old Testament passages.

It's clear that Mary didn't just skim her way through Scripture. She memorized it and held it in her heart, getting to the point where it really was "living and active" and "sharper than any double-edged sword" (Hebrews 4:12). The same can be true for us, if only we'd get Scripture off the pages of our Bible and running through our blood. Would life ever really be the same again if we managed this? Why not make a commitment today to learn more of the Bible? How good would it be to be able to know it, live it, and breathe it, so that what pours out of us is God's Word, pure and simple—whether we are on the streets or facing times of great excitement, challenge, temptation, or failure?

I've got a feeling that one of the key reasons Mary was chosen for this amazing task was that she loved God's Word. And from the moment she became a mother to God's child, she showed her child how to do likewise.

At her coronation Elizabeth II was presented with a Bible by the Archbishop of Canterbury—just as it has been with all the kings and queens of the British Commonwealth. As he presented it, he uttered these words: "Your Majesty, here are the lively oracles of God, the most precious thing this life affords."

And that's the truth. We might not spend much time getting into the Bible, and we might completely forget to treat it with the respect it's due, but it really is the most precious thing on the planet. It's the only thing I know of that contains the keys to a worthwhile life here on earth and an eternal one to come. We might want to be used by God for high and holy purposes that last forever, but without immersing ourselves in God's Word, we're never going to make it. It is this, and not our own man-sized dreams and visions, that must direct our plans.

The last thing to stand out, as we look at this passage right at the start of Jesus' life on earth, is Mary's humility. Her song isn't full of arrogance or ego but humility and sacrifice instead. It reminds me a lot of David's song when he was dragged out of obscurity as a shepherd boy to rule a nation:

> Who am I, O Sovereign LORD, and what is
> my family, that you have brought me this far?

> And as if this were not enough in your sight,
> O Sovereign LORD, you have also spoken
> about the future of the house of your servant.
> Is this your usual way of dealing with man, O
> Sovereign LORD? (2 Samuel 7:18–19)

Of course the answer is yes—it is exactly God's usual way of dealing with men and women. Reading the Bible, I get the feeling God just loves to stun the humble with his awesome intervention.

Gideon was the least in the lowest family but went on to defeat the Midianites. Amos the gardener made his status clear with these words:

> I was neither a prophet nor a prophet's son,
> but I was a shepherd, and I also took care
> of sycamore-fig trees. But the LORD took
> me from tending the flock and said to me,
> "Go, prophesy to my people Israel." (Amos
> 7:14–15)

There are others, too, and I love every single story. But it's more than mere entertainment or good drama. If you and I will get to the place where God really does get all the glory—like Mary, David,

Gideon, and Amos—then maybe we'll find ourselves involved in greater things than we've experienced so far.

One thing I'm sure of is that right now the Lord's eyes continue to range the earth. He's not on the hunt for talent, giftedness, or sexiness; just a humble heart and a life willing to react quickly and obediently to his Word. When he comes across that, he'll strongly support it. You won't find yourself giving birth in the way that Mary did, but you will give birth to some God-sized visions for your community. Bit by bit you will stop living a life plagued by small-minded and insular views. Instead you will live large, bearing the fruit that he chose for you on the day he went out of his way to select you for eternal life.

Ephesians 2:10 makes this absolutely clear: "We are God's workmanship, created in Christ Jesus to do good works, which God prepared in advance for us to do." Maybe some years in the future, when old age has settled upon you, you might be able to inch a little closer to saying to God, "I've brought you glory by completing most of the work you gave me to do."

Isn't that really what life is all about?

HOPE REFLECTED

1. If someone looked at your bank statements, Internet-browser history, or phone records, what would he or she say are your priorities? Try doing the exercise yourself or—if you're brave enough—give someone else permission to do it for you.

2. What place does the Bible have in your head and heart? Do you know it? Do you like it? Do you feel as though you need it to help you through the day? If you've answered no to any of those, don't worry or feel condemned, but do make up your mind to do something about it. Talk to someone at church who is wise and trustworthy and who knows the Bible. Ask him or her to help you get to know it better.

3. Are you feeling as though everyone else has a God-given calling and you do not? Are you still waiting for God to deliver you a dream that matches your hopes and expectations? Stop. Think back over the last seventy-two hours: Have there been times when you have ignored things that God may have been prompting you to do? Are there conversations you avoided, situations you backed out of, or things you simply ignored? If so, you need to repent and rediscover a

little more obedience. Or are you struggling to think of anything that God might have been speaking to you about? If that's the case, you need to know this: God doesn't stay silent for long. Talk to someone about how you can learn to hear him better.

4. Humility is a hard thing to measure—particularly in ourselves. But it's worth having a go. Are there people or places or tasks that— deep down—you know you go out of your way to avoid? Are there areas of your life that you've fenced off from God? Are there dreams and ambitions that you can't let go of? If so, take a look back at Mary's reaction to her unexpected pregnancy. How do you think she would respond in your situation?

2

NOT FLUFFY BUNNIES OR FACEBOOK

Luke 4:16–19

I'm a ministry geek. Every now and then I like to look at what others are up to and see what makes them tick. If they can teach me what makes them successful in reaching and keeping people for Jesus, then I'm all ears.

As I grew up, there was no ministry that could even come close to the success of the Billy Graham Evangelistic Association. Not only did they have millions coming forward in response to Billy's appeals, but they also saw great success in supporting committed disciples. On the back of his original and legendary Haringey Crusades in the 1950s, the British Bible Colleges were bombarded with men and women offering themselves for ordination. Okay, you could argue that deciding to become a full-time minister isn't necessarily the ultimate sign of discipleship, but at least it showed that something big was going on.

I committed my life to Christ in 1977, and around that time, if you asked any gathering of adults how they came to faith, the name Billy Graham would be mentioned more than any other. Today in many nations that position has been replaced by Alpha, the course born out of Holy Trinity Brompton in London that offers a basic introduction to Christianity. More than two million people in the United Kingdom have been through it, and multiple millions more in almost every country in the world have experienced it firsthand. As a result numerous people have come to faith, and by the very nature of the course they have had the opportunity to be introduced to loving Christian communities.

Recently a member of my family said—completely out of the blue—"You know what, Andy? I'd quite like to do that Alpha course." I tried to stay calm while my heart was jumping.

"Okay. Let's take a look at their Web site."

We sat down and searched. Once you've narrowed your country selection down from 163 options (from Afghanistan to Zimbabwe), you then get to the part where you add your postcode (or zip code). We put it in and found nine Alpha courses just about to start within a couple of miles of her house in South Manchester. That's nine out of more than thirty thousand courses taking place in every corner of the planet.

So are there are any parallels between these two very different approaches to mission, both of which God has seen fit to bless more than just about any other ministry at work over the past couple of generations? I think there is something important that these two ministries have in common, and that is the role played by friendship. Billy Graham started out in the late 1940s with his friends Cliff Barrows (who himself was a quality evangelist) leading his worship, George Beverly Shea doing a solo, and a group of guys including T. W. Wilson handling things behind the scenes. At his final event, Billy came on to preach after the rock bands had done their thing. Guess who his team was? Cliff, George, T. W., and company. From all accounts you couldn't meet a more devoted group of brothers.

Similarly the Alpha team is first and foremost a bunch of friends who came out of university together sharing a dream. Nicky and Pippa Gumbel, Nicky and Sila Lee, and Ken Costa have worked together and ducked and dived to spread Alpha all over the world. They all came under the leadership of Sandy Millar. For about twenty years Nicky Gumbel was in a singular position: at the same time as being one of Britain's best known Christians, he was also Sandy Millar's curate—his assistant minister. He resisted the temptation to go off and set up Nicky Gumbel International Ministries. Why? Friendship. I have no doubt that God loves their commitment to word and spirit; and, yes, Nicky is a great teacher; and there are some brilliant brains behind the scenes doing all that marketing. But the main reason God seems so free to bless it is because they love each other. God himself lives in perfect community, as Father, Son, and Holy Spirit, and he longs to be our friend. Jesus said, "I no longer call you servants, because a servant does not know his master's business. Instead, I have called you friends" (John 15:15).

It's the same when I go to the Soul Survivor festivals. They have grown to be by far the largest in Europe and involve thousands of young people coming to Jesus every year, yet there are no big-name speakers. As far as I can see, the events are led by a bunch of that guy Mike Pilavachi's friends.

Do you get my message? God loves friendship. We're not talking about fluffy bunnies or Facebook here; when Christians work out what it means to love, serve, and cheer one another on, then the results make people stop and think.

Allow me to become Mr. Ministry Geek again. The largest Christian mission agency right now isn't Billy Graham's, Alpha, or Soul Survivor, but Campus Crusade for Christ. It was started in 1951 by Bill Bright and a few of his friends, with the purpose of reaching out to their university campuses. Now they have over 25,000 staff and work in 191 countries. Next up is Youth With A Mission, with over 16,000 staff working in 149 countries. YWAM was started in 1960 by a young man called Loren Cunningham and—you guessed it—two of his friends. They started out in his mom's spare bedroom, trying to work out a way to reach the young people of their area through words and action.

The message is simple: If you want to reach out for Jesus, don't just form a mission committee; find some friends and *stay* friends through thick and thin! Throughout the last two thousand years, the greatest hindrance to world mission has been Christians disagreeing and splitting off into tens of thousands of competing factions, all in spite of the fact that Jesus' great prayer for us was that we would be "brought to complete unity to let the world know that you sent me and have loved them even as you have loved me" (John 17:23). The real success of the first church in Acts 2, where "the Lord added to their number daily those who were being saved," was built on the foundation that "all the believers were together and had everything in common" (verses 44, 47).

Of course unity and friendship are so much harder to achieve in reality than on paper. It takes huge doses of grace and the power of the Spirit to really connect with others, but I reckon far too much is at stake not to work harder than ever at it. Don't you?

I've never met Loren Cunningham or Bill Bright (who is now in heaven), but I was recently told of a time in 1975 when Loren was on holiday vacation in Colorado. He'd just received a vision from the Lord of seven mountains of culture that need to be taken by the church of Jesus if we are truly to get the job done. As he prayed, he felt that he received insight into the ways in which people could be discipled: in the home and family; education; religion; media; government; sports, entertainment, and the arts; and commerce. These were the areas to which he felt God was pointing him. Loren then discovered that Bill Bright from Campus Crusade for Christ and his wife, Vonette, were also on holiday vacation in Colorado, and so the next day they agreed to meet up. Loren reached into his coat pocket and pulled out the notes he'd written down after praying. Bill did the same. Both men had received the same vision—same mountains, same areas, same direction.

Our job isn't primarily to get people to come to church. They will want to do that when the church wakes up to the fact that we have been sent out to build God's kingdom. When we go into the areas of home and family; education; religion; media; government; sports, entertainment, and the arts; and commerce, in the power of the Spirit, demonstrating the kindness of God and boldly sharing the good news, that's when we'll see the lines of people outside the church doors.

Let's get back to the gospel of Luke. In chapter 4 we see that Jesus had a time of praying, fasting, and looking to his Father before unveiling his mission strategy. This lasted forty days and took place in the desert. Up to this time we know very little of what happened to Jesus, except that he "grew in wisdom and stature, and in favor with God and men" (2:52). Then, as soon as he was baptized, Jesus heard these wonderful words: "You are my Son, whom I love; with you I am well pleased" (3:22).

Think about it. At this point, as far as we know, Jesus had not preached a single message, healed a single sick person, or cast out a single demon, yet his Father just loved him all the same. The same is true of you and me. We don't plan to reach out to earn God's favor; we've already got it big-time. We act and speak and go out into the world as a grateful response to his great love.

Back in the desert: Jesus was there to receive his calling and to fight with the Devil. The Bible says Jesus was "full of the Holy Spirit" (Luke 4:1), but thirteen verses and forty days later he was "in the power of the Spirit" (verse 14). Between the words *full of* and *in the power of* there is a significant difference. As it did with Jesus, the power of the Spirit tends to kick in once we move out into community and put into action our plans to bless and help people in his name.

These days we seem to spend inordinate amounts of time waiting to be filled in our meetings, but getting filled in meetings is not what we need. We have to be moving in the power of the Spirit, and I believe that tends to come as we take the good news outside our churches. You can see it with the disciples; they all got their fill in the upper room with those tongues of fire, the room shaking, and everyone speaking in new languages (Acts 2). If that happened nowadays, there would be plenty of people who wanted to get on a plane to see if they could catch some of the blessing, bag it, and bring it home. But what happened in Acts was right, and it didn't involve more and more people crowding into the room to feel good about the cozy clique they were creating. All that power and blessing didn't hem them in—it drove them out! They were compelled to carry it outside, down the few steps and into the sight of the masses. Three thousand people came to know Jesus, and in the process a movement was born that would turn the world upside down. That's the kind of power we need to see.

As we know, Jesus came out of the desert in the power of the Spirit to read Isaiah 61 in the synagogue. I would have loved to be there. The Bible tells us that every eye was fastened on him. I reckon all the little kids went quiet; even the goats and chickens were silenced as he read:

> The Spirit of the Lord is on me, because he has
> anointed me to preach good news to the poor.
> He has sent me to proclaim freedom for the
> prisoners and recovery of sight for the blind,

to release the oppressed, to proclaim the year
of the Lord's favor. (Luke 4:18–19)

For the next couple of years these words drove him forward,
leaving the synagogue and embarking upon the most extraordinary
mission the world has ever seen.

If these words help define the model that Jesus worked to, then
surely they ought to have some kind of impact on our lives as we
try to follow Jesus? So it is good to ask questions about how much
the poor, the prisoners, and the oppressed feature in our plans. Can
we find these people near us? Have they experienced firsthand our
bold preaching, great acts of kindness, sacrifice, and service? Are
they more aware of the miraculous nature of God because of our
presence?

If the answer is no, then maybe we aren't actually following Jesus
as much as we thought we were. It's not enough for our churches
to endure the years or to be good at enticing other Christians from
their home churches. We need leaders who will step out in faith,
not for the latest building project so that the in-crowd can have
a more comfortable time when they come to church, but for the
lost, harassed, and helpless people they rub shoulders with every
day. Regardless of whether we live in tough communities like those
Eden workers or in comfortable suburbia like the majority, there
are great oceans of people around us who have heard, seen, or felt
too little of the love of God simply because we have been too busy
filling up and locking ourselves in at church.

Sorry. That was a bit of a rant. However, someone needs to say how crazy and unbiblical the way we do church so often is.

I was flicking through a book on mission. I was enjoying it, right up to the section about budgeting. The suggested structure for a church was this: personnel 50 percent, facilities 20 percent, programming 20 percent, and finally mission 10 percent!

What is that all about? Mission is not the added extra we throw a few coins at when we have done everything else we need to do. It's the main thing; it's our core, our *raison d'être*. Alongside knowing Jesus there is simply nothing more important than making him known in words and actions. If only leaders who know in their hearts that this is true would plan their church budgets and activities accordingly! If that happened, then some of those Christians who have been red-hot in the past would rise up again and rearrange their own priorities. Once more we'd be making the main thing the main thing, putting our faith out there in word and action.

I know of a church who started to do that. Every month they gave each of their home groups £100 (about $150) and instructed them to use it creatively in blessing their communities. All sorts of great things happened. Homes were decorated, homeless people were fed, boxes of chocolates and flowers were delivered to every home just to be generous for the sake of it. And on the back of all this kindness, people had amazing fun. And guess what: The church has grown. Phenomenally.

I was at a church-planting conference and was interested when, quite independently, two of the teams said that a key part of their strategy for church planting was healing on the streets. Their plan was simple—to sensitively ask people if they would appreciate prayer for healing. Both teams explained that they had seen remarkable healings week after week, the kind they have never seen in their services. It reminded me of another set of stories from a large city church. There were some great stories of healing, but they all seemed to have happened on the way home from church after the meeting had finished. Do you think God might be saying something to us?

Someone has said that when it comes to taking the message out to people, if you bring a thimble to God, he fills it; if you bring a bucket, he fills that, too. At the back of my mind is this: What if I bring him a bathtub? At The Message we have been mighty busy with all sorts of plans to unleash acts of kindness, and our teams have delivered community action projects right across the region. However, this year I knew we needed to marry it with preaching the good news more than ever before. So we raised our game in the field of bold proclamation. We stepped out in faith and took on two new mission teams, and we approached more schools and local churches to partner with us than ever before. We also went across the region and booked the largest rock venues every month for huge gigs with a clear gospel message and an opportunity to respond. As a result at least twice as many young people have come to faith this year than ever before, and tens of thousands of teenagers across our city have been presented with the good news in a relevant way.

Hope '08 was a wonderful UK-wide initiative that brought almost 1,500 regional groups together. I was heavily involved with it and loved the message we united under: Do More, Do It Together, and Do It in Words and Actions. Right at the start of the adventure I went on a tour to bang the drum with that man Mike Pilavachi and the Soul Survivor team. In the afternoon we would share the vision with leaders and then invite any questions. One leader who obviously had the ministry of encouragement said, "How do you know it isn't going to be a massive flop like so many of these national initiatives?" He then went on to list about sixteen different attempts to do something on a national scale here in the United Kingdom, none of which had amounted to much. I felt myself shrinking back into my chair, until Mike weighed in: "Well, if we are going to go down, let's go down trying to reach people for Jesus."

There is honestly no other option but to keep stepping out in faith to make Jesus known. Mike had nailed it. Suddenly, I was joining in and getting all excited. The poor leader had probably just had a bad day, and by now he was shrinking back in *his* chair. Of course, he did have a point: Why bother if we aren't going to get into God's presence and get his heart before ducking and diving to make him known? But once we've made up our minds to serve God and give it our all, should we really let anything get in our way?

HOPE REFLECTED

1. What do you think would happen if you and a group of friends—or your home group—decided to give away £100 ($150) a month for the next six months? Do you think you could help people? Do you think it would be a good way of showing the love of God? Do you think it would make a difference? If you've answered yes to any of these, why not do it? And if you really believe in it, why not find the money among yourselves?

2. Where does friendship rank on your list of priorities? Does it cost you your time, your money, and your energy, even when you're running low? What could you do in the next twenty-four hours to show appreciation and support for your friends?

3. Are you discouraged? If you were to write two lists, one of all the things that haven't worked out in your life and one of all the things that have, which would be longer? What part does God play in either? Do you blame him or take credit yourself? Are there areas of your life that you need to look at again and allow God to change?

4. What kind of container do you approach God with? Are you a thimble holder or more of a bucket person? How much transformation among your friends and community do you believe is possible? How much do you expect God can do and will do? What part are you willing to play in it all? Ask God to open your eyes, head, hands, and heart to the full extent of his potential.

3

GETTING INTO THE BOAT

Luke 4:29—5:11

Things come and go in all aspects of life, and it's no different when it comes to the seasons of the Spirit. Doing what I do—preaching, networking, and dreaming up the vision—there seem to be times when you can't put a foot wrong. These are the "open heaven" times, with loads of people coming to faith, new opportunities and connections, tons of new and imaginative ideas, and even some great healing stories to tell. I've been there and it's great; it's like kingdom come.

Then there are times when it's as if you're wading through mud. You preach your heart out and get no response. The sick leave you feeling disappointed. You struggle to raise money and you can't come up with a good idea to save your life. I suppose that's just the way it is this side of heaven, but I can't help feeling frustrated by it.

It doesn't help when I remember that Jesus never seemed to experience this ebb and flow in anointing or that he said we would do even greater things than he did. Yes, I know he had desperate times of discouragement and disappointment and even despair, but still every person he prayed for seemed to be healed. His life led to the most outrageous multiplication of kingdom activity, and before he left this earth he gave us the Holy Spirit, saying, "As the Father has sent me, I am sending you" (John 20:21). With all this going right for Jesus and there being so many times when it seems as though everything's going stale for us, it makes me wonder: Are we missing something? If we just prayed a little harder, fasted a little more often, took ourselves off on a few more retreats, or hit the streets with greater commitment … wouldn't life be different?

As Jesus left the synagogue, it's clear that he was a man the likes of which the world had never seen before. His preaching had a massive authority that could either switch people off so much that they wanted to kill him (Luke 4:29) or switch them on so much that they were utterly amazed (Luke 4:36). News about his life and work traveled throughout the area. He confronted the powers of darkness and cast out demons with a simple "be quiet" and "come out." As for illness and disease, these were healed simply by laying his hands on the people in question. It's obvious that he was really on a roll. There was nothing stopping him from preaching the good news of the kingdom, healing the sick, and caring for the poor and the marginalized. It seemed like he needed no one, as if he'd got it all perfectly in order and would just carry on showing the world what God is really like.

So why did he go and spoil it all by letting a bunch of fishermen join in? He must have known that they had the potential to mess everything up, so why bother? The answer? Because that's what our God always does. His first thought is one of partnership—even partnership with fickle, inconsistent individuals like you and me and those first disciples.

In Luke 5, as Jesus wandered around the lake working out the mission the Father had given him, he was on the lookout for recruits for this inner circle. He was hunting down the very men in whom he would invest, prior to releasing them right across the world to do exactly what he'd been doing by the power of the Spirit.

Jesus was always thinking on his feet and being creative. When he wanted to reach people, he got on their level and spoke in their language. (If only his church could be a bit better at these two things, what a difference we would make!) So, as people began to crowd around him, desperate for a touch and a word, he improvised. Around the shores of Lake Galilee were steep inlets and caves, which meant that if you could find a little boat and push out from the shore a bit, you would have natural amplification as your voice traveled much farther than normal. Little did Simon Peter know, as he agreed to lend Jesus his boat for this purpose, that he was about to be swept off his feet by what Jesus had to say.

Wouldn't you love to have been there? How much would you give to have heard the master communicator bring the words of eternal life from Simon Peter's little boat to that crowd? I'm guessing that as he spoke Jesus had one eye on the guy sitting there at his feet, lapping it all up. Even now Jesus would have spotted that Simon Peter was more than a little like Rocky: a big-hearted, generous, large-mouthed guy who was just what the Father was looking for to lead this new kingdom movement.

So Jesus broke off from his preaching and invited Simon Peter to put out into deep water for some fishing. A nice idea, fishing with the Son of God … except for the fact that the middle of the day is a horrible time for fishing. In the baking heat of the Middle East all the little fishes move to the cooler waters at the bottom of the lake. In fact on this occasion there were no fish around at all, as Simon Peter was quick to point out. They had fished all night and caught nothing—frustrating enough when you are supposed to be good at fishing, but more than frustrating when your livelihood depends on it.

But Jesus, the amateur fisherman, suggested they have a go, so Simon Peter said through gritted teeth, "Because you say so, I will let down the nets." Against all the odds—at the wrong time of day and after a night of nothing—"they caught such a large number of fish that their nets began to break. So they signaled their partners in the other boat to come and help them, and they came and filled both boats so full that they began to sink" (Luke 5:5–7).

I love this story. It tells us so much about our own attempts to be "fishers of men." First, through all our labors, even working all night, we are not going to see anyone come to know Jesus. We don't have the power. That's God's business. We have to put our nets out, but it's only God who can fill them. And yes, there are times when we get everything right—we're prayed up well, we're flamed and passionate—and yet we still catch nothing. Why? These are the times when God is busy teaching us a precious lesson about utter dependence on him. Have you ever thought that it was just as much of a miracle for absolutely no fish to be caught all night by professional fishermen as it was for the nets to be bulging the next morning?

Sometimes Jesus is at work even in our disappointment. What seem to us to be failures and fruitless efforts are ready to be transformed into something even more valuable.

I remember well the first citywide mission that my brother and I organized. It was called Message '88 and was a totally wacky step of faith for two young businessmen who were not at all well known in church circles. Still, we had a heart to reach young people.

We booked the biggest rock venue in the city for a week and worked hard with local churches for eighteen months in the buildup. On the first night we had a great time—with bands, theater companies, celebrity testimonies, and, best of all, loads of young people. At the end of the night I preached my heart out. How many came to faith? None. We'd done everything right and yet our nets were completely empty. Instead of seeing it as a lesson in the making, I was gutted. Is there anything worse after you have preached than going into an empty response room and hearing people say things like, "Don't worry, brother, it's not about numbers"? Of course it's about numbers! God wanted every one of those young people to come to faith, and I was with him. But, just as with Simon Peter, it wasn't happening.

At times like that there are only two options: Give up or carry on. If you go for the second option, you pray more and believe that things will get better. Now, because we'd spent a lot of money, the first option wasn't even on the table for us. So we carried on, and it wasn't long before the same bands, theater companies, and preachers saw a massive response, with loads of young people coming to faith. By the weekend the faithful response team who had been twiddling their thumbs on the previous Monday were running around looking for partners who would help them manage the overflow of people.

Of course we should never really consider giving up on preaching and living the gospel out. This is why Paul challenged timid Timothy to "preach the Word … in season and out of season" and "do the work of an evangelist" (2 Timothy 4:2, 5).

Back in Luke 5 this was exactly what Simon the fisherman needed. He knew all about fish, and he knew what a miracle this midday catch was. It was the kind of thing only God could do, so right there in the boat he fell on his knees, with the fish flip-flopping around him, and said, "Go away from me, Lord; I am a sinful man!" (verse 8).

Simon's words bring to mind another famous encounter with the Lord, some seven centuries earlier, as recorded in Isaiah 6. That was the time when, before he chose to walk on the earth, God turned up in the temple in glory, seated on a throne high and exalted, with the train of his robe filling the temple. All the angels were singing so loud that they literally shook the temple to its foundations. Isaiah's response is no surprise: "Woe to me! … I am ruined! For I am a man of unclean lips … and my eyes have seen the King, the LORD Almighty" (verse 5).

The Lord responded to Isaiah's worshipping in brokenness and humility pretty much the same way he did to Simon Peter's. He said, "Whom shall I send? And who will go for us?"

Isaiah responded, "Here am I. Send me!" and then heard the commissioning words: "Go and tell this people ..." (Isaiah 6:8–9).

For Simon Peter on his knees in the boat the words were "Don't be afraid; from now on you will catch men" (Luke 5:10). So he pulled up the boats—presumably still full of fish—left everything, and followed Jesus.

Real worship always takes place in humility. We can't simply cruise up to our mighty God pretending we are good enough. We must be awestruck and sometimes overwhelmed by his glory and generosity. And then we see that real worship always results in more mission; it always sends us out. We have not really worshipped the Lord until we have gotten to the place that Isaiah and Simon Peter and millions of other believers down the centuries reached, where they just can't stand the fact that God is not getting all the glory he deserves. They know they have to do something to put it right.

Real worship also results in sacrifice. For both Simon Peter and Isaiah the cost was high. Both men were ultimately killed for leaving everything and following their calling. We believe Simon Peter was crucified upside down and Isaiah was sawed in half. For us it may not mean anything as bloody as that, but at the very least, to be successful fishers of men will involve great sacrifice of our timetables and personal treasures.

What a day Simon Peter had! He started out frustrated by his night's work, probably wondering what the point of being a fisherman was if there were no fish to catch, and he ended it leaving everything and embarking on this dangerous, exciting, fruitful mission adventure. He started out self-employed and ended up with the Son of God in charge of his every moment. As a result of his obedience literally billions of people have been blessed.

As we get serious about our calling, let's make no bones about it: It will be costly, and we will need to reorder our lives and our priorities so that fishing for men is at the top of the list. Of course this makes absolute sense when, as Blaise Pascal said, people are the only thing we can take with us when we leave this earth. How glad is Simon Peter right now, in eternity, as he realizes that his faithful and sometimes painful service has been rewarded with such a vast catch?

Finally, a story. It would probably be funny if it wasn't so painfully true:

> Now it came to pass that a group existed who called themselves fishermen. There were many fish in the waters all around. Week after week, month after month, and year after year, the fishermen met in meetings and talked about their call to fish, the abundance of fish and how they might go about fishing.

Year after year, they carefully defined what fishing means, defended fishing as an occupation, declared that fishing is always to be a primary task of fishermen—in fact, that there should be a Decade of Fishing!

Continually they searched for new and better methods of fishing. Further they said, "The fishing industry exists by fishing as fire exists by burning." They loved slogans such as "Fishing is the task of every fisherman," and "Every fisherman is a fisher." They sponsored costly nationwide and worldwide congresses to discuss fishing issues such as new fishing equipment, fish calls, and whether any new bait had been discovered.

Many who felt the call to be fishermen responded. They were commissioned and sent to fish. They engaged in all kinds of occupations. They built power plants to pump water for fish and tractors to plough new waterways. They made all kinds of equipment to travel here and there to look at fish hatcheries. Some also said that they wanted to be part of a fishing party, but they felt called to furnish fishing equipment. Others felt their job was to relate to the fish in a good way so the fish would know the difference between good and bad fishermen. Others felt that simply letting the fish know they were nice, land-loving neighbours and how loving and kind they were was enough.

These fishermen built large beautiful buildings called "Fishing Headquarters." The plea was that everyone should be a fisherman and should fish. One thing they didn't do, however—they didn't fish.

After one stirring meeting on "The necessity of fishing," one young man left the meeting and went fishing. The next day he reported that he had caught two fish. He was honoured for his excellent catch and scheduled to visit all the big meetings possible to tell how he did it. So he left his fishing in order to have time to tell other fishermen about the experience. He was also placed on the Fishermen's General Board as a person having considerable experience.

Now it's true that many of the fishermen
sacrificed and put up with all kinds of difficul-
ties. Some lived near the water and bore the
smell of dead fish every day. They received the
ridicule of some who made fun of their fishermen's clubs and the fact that they claimed
to be fishermen yet never fished. They won-
dered about those who felt it was of little use
to attend the weekly meetings to talk about
fishing. After all, were they not following the
Master who said, "Follow me and I will make
you fishers of men"?

—*Quoted in J. John and Mark Stibbe,*
A Box of Delights *(Monarch, 2001)*

HOPE REFLECTED

1. Generally we do not like to be told too much about the cost of discipleship. And there is a balance to be found—between realizing what we get as well as what we give up. How are your scales on this? Do you lean heavily in either direction, perhaps getting overwhelmed with the burden or responsibility, or do you go in the other direction and perhaps not take things seriously enough? Take time to think, pray, and talk to someone you trust. Are there things you need to let go of? Do you need to learn to trust God a little more? Do you need to take some more risks?

2. Have you had one of those encounters with Jesus—the sort that reminds us of Isaiah's and Simon Peter's? Have you been struck by just how great God is and how unworthy we are? Remind yourself what it felt like, or ask God to reveal it to you for the first time.

3. The book of Isaiah relates to more than the people the prophet was talking to. Take time to read it all the way through, making notes if you like of things that relate to Jesus in particular. What would Isaiah be saying if he were alive today and living near you?

4. When was the last time you went through a difficult period of faith? What were the symptoms? What helped? What did you learn? Perhaps you're going through one of those periods right now. Does anyone else know this about you? Tell someone you trust and take time as often as possible to read Scripture, to think, and to pray. Expect to hear from God.

4

A QUESTION OF HEALING

Luke 5:12–26

Sandwiched between the introductions of working-class fishermen and a dodgy tax collector, Luke 5 really contains two amazing miracles and some wonderful salvation, as Jesus continues to model just what it means to follow him.

Recently I went with a few friends into a hospital to visit some patients. We were trying to follow Jesus but somehow felt as though our steps were too small. We were visiting and praying with a thirteen-year-old boy who was dying of AIDS. His mother wept by his bedside. We mustered up all the faith we could and prayed in the name of Jesus. We were desperate to see the boy healed. It didn't happen. The following day I visited a faithful old pastor who had gone blind. Again, I prayed for a miracle of healing yet left the man still in the dark. I went to bed that night feeling frustrated with God.

Why is it so hard to see major healing miracles? How is it that prayer to find a lost mobile phone can work, while pleading for a boy with AIDS does nothing at all? The phone turned up; the boy died. It just seems so wrong.

You cannot get away from the fact that if we are meant to follow Jesus and walk in his steps, then we're right to look out for healing miracles. But it's my experience that too often they simply do not happen.

Let me nail my colors to the mast. I still expect to see healing today. In fact I've got some great healing stories myself. I remember on one occasion preaching in a church and at the end of the service asking people if they would like to go into a side room to pray with someone and receive Christ as Lord and Savior. It was great as a number of young people came through, and I had the privilege of leading a girl to Jesus. She had the look of someone who had been battered by life. After we'd prayed together and it was obvious that she meant business, I asked her if there was anything else she would appreciate prayer for. She shocked me by saying yes. She explained that her life was plagued by epileptic fits. She would have three or four a day and had to go to a special school. I gulped hard but told her that I would pray.

"I'm going to pray for healing," I said, "and I believe that one of three things will happen: from right now you will have no more fits; or the fits will gradually become less and less; or they will continue but God will give you great strength to cope." You could say I was hedging my bets and that it wasn't the most faith-filled explanation, but I prayed for her healing and off she went.

A couple of years later I was involved in a school's mission in her part of the world, and at the end-of-the-week concert the same girl came up to me. But I had to do a double take because she looked completely different. The hardness and bitterness had gone, and I knew there and then that God had been working in her life.

For about ten minutes we had a great conversation as she explained how she had joined a church and was walking with Jesus. I was delighted but was also desperate to know how she had been getting on with her epileptic fits. Eventually I plucked up the courage and asked her. She answered by saying, "Oh, I haven't had a single one since."

How wonderful is that? But of course I'm left feeling glad for her while at the same time wondering why the same God who was able to do that can't also heal the boy with AIDS. Or the blind pastor.

Perhaps Luke 5 can help us understand this tricky business a bit more. In verse 17, it says something fascinating: As Jesus was teaching the Pharisees and the teachers of the law, "the power of the Lord was present for him to heal the sick." Isn't it logical to conclude, then, that if there were times when the power to heal was present, there might also have been times when that same power was not present? And we have that extraordinary statement in Mark 6:5–6 that Jesus "could not do any miracles there … and he was amazed at their lack of faith."

I've become convinced that God does heal and will heal today. But sometimes, on this side of heaven, God's power is specially present for healing … and sometimes it's not. What also seems true is that when we spend time in God's presence and have more faith, the periods when the healing power is present happen more often—they are more powerful and more prolonged. This is probably the reason that healings were so evident in the life of the holiest, most faith-filled man who has ever lived.

One thing's for sure: As long as we are sensitive—and maybe that's what God liked about my approach to the girl with epilepsy—the more we pray for the sick, then the more healings we will see. If we can approach things in such a way that no one is left feeling worse off, even if the power of the Lord isn't present to heal right there and then, we will be in a better place. If we are going to be followers of Jesus, then laying hands on the sick in our churches and, more important, in our communities has got to be increasingly part of the deal.

There is so much to learn from each story of these broken, sick men in Luke 5. One lesson is simple: We can be sure that Jesus is drawn to brokenness, and so should we be.

The man with leprosy in verse 12 was in a particularly bad state. In Jesus' day leper colonies were desperate places. Those who suffered with the disease were living with the hard words of Leviticus 13:45–46:

> The person with such an infectious disease must wear torn clothes, let his hair be unkempt, cover the lower part of his face and cry out, "Unclean! Unclean!" As long

> as he has the infection he remains unclean.
> He must live alone; he must live outside the
> camp.

Imagine what that does for your self-esteem. Not only had this man in Luke 5 lost his health, but also his friends, family, livelihood, and home had all been turned into memories. He was "covered" with leprosy. He was outcast, broken, filthy, and very, very sick.

Just like Simon Peter in the previous chapter, the man falls on his face before Jesus and begs him with words that say a lot about his frame of mind. He pleads, "Lord, if you are willing, you can make me clean."

"I am willing," Jesus says. "Be clean!" (verses 12–13).

We see Jesus breaking a law and reaching out and touching him—the first time in years he would have been touched. The man's appalling skin condition leaves him *immediately* (there's that word again) before their very eyes. Not only does he get new clean skin, but also his fingers and toes are restored and a sense of touch returns.

Wouldn't you love to have been there?

If I'd seen such a thing on one of our Eden projects, it definitely would have made my next newsletter. I'd be using it as a sermon illustration for weeks. Actually, for years. It probably would have had pride of place in this book too. Jesus' reaction was somewhat different.

"Don't tell anyone," he says (verse 14). It's as if at this point Jesus doesn't want to draw attention to these miracles. He doesn't want to become a traveling healing show that will detract from his main purpose of preaching the good news of the kingdom and showing people the way to eternal life.

There is a lot for us here. Yes we must pray for the sick, and yes we must engage in all manner of kindness, but we must never lose sight of the gospel perspective, communicating in words and actions that everyone can understand and expecting a response wherever we go.

In Mark 1:38, when Jesus is experiencing the power of God to heal in the most amazing measure and thousands are flocking to him, his response is to say, "Let us go somewhere else." He heads off to the nearby villages so that he can preach there, too. His job—and our job too—was first and foremost to preach, to expand people's minds so that they could fully understand the importance and the possibility of having a relationship with him. Just delivering acts of kindness—or even just seeing great healing miracles—would be to sell people short. We have to introduce people to the whole range of healing, the whole breadth of kindness that comes only from truly knowing God.

As the news about the extraordinary miracles grew and the buzz spread that maybe Jesus really was the one they'd been waiting for, huge crowds followed him wherever he went. People turned up to hear his teaching and experience the miraculous acts that flowed from his being. Earlier we saw him shouting across the hillsides to the thousands, but in Luke 5, Jesus set camp in a small house in Capernaum and started teaching. For the people there, the immediate good news was that the power of God was present to heal. It would be like U2, Radiohead, or Coldplay deciding to do the next gig of their national arena tour in the local village hall. Chaos would reign, with thousands of people crowding outside with no chance of getting near the main event.

It was especially frustrating for one paralyzed man who had been brought by his friends with the expectation that this could be the day that changed his life (Luke 5:18–19). But his friends weren't about to give up. They made their way up the steps that were at the side of most Middle Eastern homes in Jesus' day and started smashing their way through the compressed mud and straw roof. At first, Jesus' teaching was interrupted by a bit of banging and then, I imagine, some dust dropped on his head, followed by great lumps of mud and straw. Eventually a hole opened up in the ceiling large enough to lower a man through. I don't think the person who offered his house to Jesus for this meeting expected this! But make no mistake, Jesus always puts people before possessions—whether it's two thousand pigs or our precious homes. Jesus loves people … especially desperate, broken people.

You can imagine the hush that descended in the house as the crowd cleared and the crippled man was lowered on his mat. As the dust settled, excitement mounted. Surely they were about to witness another miracle. But Jesus shocked them all, offending the Pharisees and teachers of the law by looking at the man and saying, "Friend, your sins are forgiven" (verse 20). As far as we know, the man wasn't asking for forgiveness; he just wanted healing. But the Friend of sinners could see right into his heart and knew his greatest need was freedom from sin. In one sense, what was the point of healing him from paralysis, if in a few years' time he would be marching straight into hell because of his sin?

But then, as we know, to prove he really was the one who is able to forgive sins once and for all, Jesus told the man to get up, take his mat, and go home. Immediately, we are told, he stood up in front of them and went home praising God. That's an understatement in the extreme! What a day: dropped through a roof, forgiven of sins, healed of paralysis. Don't you love what Jesus did for him and for the guy with leprosy? He's still doing it today, still bringing people back to him as they put their faith in him.

Our true desperation and main desire must always be to see the greatest miracle of all take place in our communities. Before even comforting the dying or healing the sick, we have the joy of dispensing the miracle of forgiveness liberally in our communities, through bold proclamation of the good news. Doctors can share in the physical miracles, but the restoration of relationship with God is truly out of their hands.

There are many churches who tend to be good at one thing—maybe preaching or moving in the miraculous or social engagement. But is it enough to be good at just one part? That's not how champions operate. In sport, the good players are destroyed by the great ones. The lesser players tend to excel at just one part of their game. But the true greats have it all. If they or their coaches detect the slightest sign of weakness, they work tirelessly on that area to perfect it.

Shouldn't this be our approach? Can we settle for less? How can we hope to do great things for Jesus unless we find ways to deliver bold words, great kindness, *and* an expectation of the miraculous in one dynamic, world-changing mix? Isn't that the kind of church a hurting, desperate, sin-sick world needs?

HOPE REFLECTED

1. Have you prayed for healing and not seen the results you were hoping for? Do you know of others who are being prayed for at the moment but continue to be ill? What does that do to your faith? Does it leave you shaken and a little less sure of God? If so, talk about it. Talk with God about it, with your friends, and with your leaders. You should be wary of anyone who offers easy answers to these questions. Perhaps the real challenge is not working out why healing doesn't always happen but getting a bit more comfortable with not knowing everything.

2. God might not move and act in the way that we hope, but that doesn't mean we should put limits on what we think he can do. Think about how you interact with God: How much do you share with him? How many of your dreams are scripted by him, and how many are yours and yours alone? It's not all about the future either: How much of the next twenty-four hours had you planned on being God-directed? We all put limits on God, but we can all learn to release a little more of our own hold on things.

3. If the main thing is helping people form and strengthen their relationship with God, how often do you think about your involvement in this? Start by looking back on your own journey with God. Who helped you grow in faith? What did they do? How did they help steer you toward a fuller understanding of God? Were there any experiences that didn't help? Think back now: Can you apply any of the lessons to your present efforts to help others grow in their faith?

4. One coin can be enough to tip the scales, and it's the same with church. If we stop trying to balance all the tasks in front of us and choose to concentrate on one aspect alone, then we can end up far from what God intended. Who do you admire (among churches and people) who does a good job of balancing the elements that should drive the church? What would your life look like if you started to live like them a little more?

5

THE HALFTIME BREAK

Luke 7:36–50

I'm not an emotional man. Sometimes I wish I were. My wife, Michele, will weep at anything. A rerun of *The Waltons* or hearing "Seasons in the Sun" on the radio is all it takes to open up the waterworks. But not me. I didn't even cry when Manchester United won the treble.

But yesterday was different. I was in church and I found myself weeping. The preacher was talking about God's father heart, and he played a video of the legendary Dick and Rick Hoyt. Rick had a tragic accident at birth and couldn't speak or walk. He was what's called a spastic quadriplegic cerebral palsy nonspeaking person. But he refused to be defined by any such label. He was strong and determined to be included wherever possible in community life. His dad, Dick, was also determined that his son would live as normal a life as possible. He managed to convince the state to allow Rick to go to a regular school, and he found a way for Rick to communicate via a computer.

After a while Rick let his dad know he would love them to run together in the local five-mile fun run. Dick had never run in his life, but for his son he started training. He ended up pushing Rick in his wheelchair all along the course. When they reached the finish line, crowds of people were cheering them on. Both father and son had a huge sense of achievement and unity. Rick said that for the first time in his life he didn't feel disabled.

This led to them setting up Team Hoyt, taking on greater and greater challenges. Marathons, triathlons, and Ironman events all over America followed. Eventually they set about the challenge of going coast to coast across America. As I watched the video footage of Team Hoyt giving their all—running, swimming, and cycling together—something broke inside me. Maybe it was watching a father's strong, sacrificial love in action. Maybe it was seeing the power of the human spirit. Maybe it was a sense of God's great father heart for me. Whatever the reason, I was in pieces, and all because of a simple real-life story.

Jesus understood that this kind of illustration gets us. He filled his teaching with great stories about ordinary people who were just like his listeners. In Luke 7, we get one of the best, as Jesus was invited to dinner at Simon the Pharisee's house.

I love the fact that Jesus could fit in anywhere, whether it was with the social elite and their endless religious debates or with the working-class people who preferred to hear him talking about fishing and farming.

The Pharisees were the top guys in society. They would have lived in the best houses, had the best servants, and thrown the most extravagant parties. Their events were major social happenings, where people dressed up and expected to be treated royally. The first thing to happen when you arrived was for a servant to wash your feet—when you were eating reclined at the table, it was no laughing matter to have sweaty feet in your face. Next would come the olive oil, to freshen up. And finally your host would greet you with a kiss.

Except that for Jesus on this occasion, there were none of these formalities. Clearly this was no friendly invitation: Simon had invited Jesus along to trap him. To make things worse (from Simon's point of view) it seemed that all Jesus' low-life friends were hanging around the door and looking in through the windows, observing the appalling way their master was being treated.

It wasn't long before one of them broke ranks and burst into Simon's house. She was weeping as she knelt at Jesus' feet. The Bible says she was a woman who had lived a sinful life in that town. In other words, she would be well known as one of the ones to avoid. She was almost certainly a prostitute and certainly someone who wouldn't be welcome in this "holy man's" house.

In those days women would often wear their most precious possession round their necks. It was often an heirloom, handed down from generation to generation, and could be worth tens of thousands of pounds or dollars in today's money. This woman had hers with her: an alabaster jar of perfume. She now shocked everyone by breaking the jar and pouring the whole lot on Jesus' feet. It gets worse: She then undid her hair. Only dodgy women let their hair down, but here she was, massaging Jesus' feet with her tears, her precious perfume, and her hair.

It's easy to condemn Simon, but I've got a horrible feeling that if a woman of dubious pedigree did this kind of thing in my house, I'd have to think twice before I spoke. Part of me would be wondering why a truly godly man would let someone so sinful do such a thing. I'd feel embarrassed and awkward and would probably look the other way.

Jesus didn't act like that. He loved what was going on; he could see straight into the woman's heart, and he knew that this unorthodox show of affection was her way of expressing how much she loved him. Jesus knew that if she could continue to show this much public love for him in her daily life, she would be amazing. When it comes down to it, the key to a successful Christian life has to include this kind of love—the sort that doesn't care about what others think and that absorbs the very best of what you have.

When leading an organization like The Message, it's easy to bring in more and more rules to get people to do what is right, saying that we must attend certain meetings or we must pray for this long every day or we must keep the kitchen tidy or we must correspond with our personal prayer supporters. Yet even good rules like those don't work. Idealistic as it sounds, I try my best to have just one rule: Love God and do what you like. (Thanks to Saint Augustine for that one.) It worked for this woman; why can't it work for us?

Even the fact that Jesus was with the Pharisees at this point is a bit of a surprise. He had already upset them through his teaching, his social status, and probably most of all by his choice of friends. They just couldn't handle the fact that a man of God would want to be friends with con men, prostitutes, and dodgy dealers. Why wasn't he joining in with the Pharisees and condemning them?

The test remains a good one for us today. How good are we in our churches at making outsiders feel welcome, especially outsiders with all sorts of hang-ups, issues, and sins to bring with them?

Wouldn't it be great if we ended up being defined not by our stance on a particular doctrine, or even our ability to condemn sin, but by the extent to which we were great friends to the broken, messed up, and sinful people we share our lives with?

Simon's house smelled like the perfume counter at Harrods, the woman was sobbing at Jesus' feet with her hair all undone, and the party had been ruined. Inside Simon was boiling. He said to himself, "If this man were a prophet, he would know who is touching him and what kind of woman she is—that she is a sinner" (Luke 7:39). It's worth noting right here that, as far as Jesus is concerned, there is no such thing as saying something to ourselves. He sees our inmost desires and hears our inmost thoughts. As a result Jesus nailed him with verse 40: "Simon, I have something to tell you …" And that little something turns out to be utterly devastating.

Jesus told Simon the Pharisee a story of canceled debts. Two men owed money to a moneylender. One owed a week's wages, the other owed more than a year's, and neither of them had the money to pay what he owed. So the generous moneylender canceled both debts. Then Jesus asked Simon which debtor would love the moneylender most.

Simon seemed to know he was in trouble because he answered cautiously: "I suppose the one who had the bigger debt canceled."

Bingo! Jesus responded, before going on to really turn the heat up by applying the story:

> Then he turned toward the woman and said to Simon, "Do you see this woman? I came into your house. You did not give me any water for my feet, but she wet my feet with her tears and wiped them with her hair. You did not give me a kiss, but this woman, from the time I entered, has not stopped kissing my feet. You did not put oil on my head, but she has poured perfume on my feet. Therefore, I tell you, her many sins have been forgiven—for she loved much. But he who has been forgiven little loves little." (Luke 5:44–47)

Isn't it so often the case that the worst sinners really do make the best of saints? People who know they need saving are close to God's kingdom, while people who think they are okay on their own are so often miles off.

Our Eden Hattersley football team includes ex-drug dealers, gang leaders, and all the rest. They regularly play a match against a team from the Christian rehab center where, one by one, the most broken, addicted men are discovering freedom. When you first look at the two teams—complete with scars, skinheads, and tattoos—you expect all-out war. And then something amazing happens: The whistle goes and the ball starts flying around and you realize that these are guys who have been forgiven so much that they love with great depths of passion. I love it. There really is no one beyond God's grace—neither the drug dealer who drives through Hattersley with guns, nor the prostitute in the Middle East. Jesus doesn't make light of their sins, but he willingly forgives them, and don't they know it.

This willingness to forgive is what gets Jesus into trouble. Simon was doubting his credentials as a prophet, but here Jesus claimed to be someone far greater than a prophet by offering forgiveness to those in need of it. Everybody knows that only God can forgive sins. And Jesus didn't just announce the forgiveness; he told the woman what the result would be: that she could "go in peace" (Luke 7:50). My guess is that the one thing that was missing in her life was peace. It makes sense, doesn't it? Habitual sinning robs you of peace, and Jesus said that, in the place of that crushing weight of shame, rejection, and hollowness, he would pour in acceptance, joy, and *shalom*—the very word for peace that Jesus used here. It's a Bible word that means so much more than our word *peace*. It means completeness, contentedness, being right with God and right with his world. It's exactly what we need. And it's exactly what we must offer to a world that is desperate for it, whether they know it or not.

There is of course no suggestion that Simon, the religious leader, ever became a follower of Jesus. He seemed to finish the party with a harder heart than ever. Maybe he had such a grudge against Jesus after this that a few months later he was one of the Pharisees who was baying for Jesus' blood. We don't know. But we can guess what happens when we close Jesus off from our lives.

Even though most of this book is about getting out of our church buildings and going after those who don't know Jesus, I do believe in and practice getting together with other believers. The problem comes when we allow meetings to be the be-all and end-all of our Christian lives. A pastor friend of mine, Andy Hickford, has helpfully said that church gatherings are meant to be like the halftime interval in a football match. They're for us to come in from where the real action is, get patched up, and gain some instruction from our Manager so that we can do a better job in the second half when it really counts.

Perhaps the problem is that we have many churches who are characterized by having two halves of thirty seconds each and an eighty-nine-minute halftime break.

Jesus was full of grace and truth. It's been suggested that grace came first for Jesus and that it needs to come first for us. Simon's problem was that he was full of truth, but, like so many of us, it was his little versions of the truth that he cherished. His view of the world was not seasoned with the grace that makes truth palatable. He just hung on to his own bitter, narrow version of the truth.

I think there is still way too much of that in our churches today. What we need is a daily injection of the grace of Jesus—the perfect antidote to the religious spirit—as we attempt to make him known in a messed-up world.

HOPE REFLECTED

1. Who do you condemn? Whose sin do you rank higher than yours? Who would you keep from the front of church because of a sense of awkwardness or embarrassment? We all have our prejudices, but putting God's seal of approval on them simply won't do.

2. Are there people who live near your church who are not accepted by polite society? Are they poor, ill, foreign, or just plain bad? Do you think that maybe, in some way, your church might hold the potential to help introduce them to the utterly amazing love and acceptance of Jesus? Could it be more than a coincidence that you're both in the same area?

3. How much time does your church spend out on the playing field and how much back in the locker room? And what about your own life: How's the ratio? Do you spend more time talking than doing? Or maybe you're forever out on the playing field, unhappy at the thought of coming back in and getting a pep talk from the Manager. Either way, things don't have to be like this.

4. What does it mean to you to be "religious"? Some people find the term unhelpful; others are more relaxed with it. The important question is this: What are the characteristics that define your life as a Christian? Is it the way you follow the rules, your knowledge of structure, your position of authority? Or is it your appreciation of God's grace, your time spent at his feet, and bringing others in to meet him?

6

I NEVER LIKED THE FLOOR THAT MUCH ANYWAY

Luke 8:1–15

I love the way that Jesus did whatever it took to get people to understand the good news of the kingdom of God. (Have I told you that before?) The way he crafted stories that were laced with a God-twist always leaves me stunned by their simple genius. He was able to leave the words hanging in the air, with the crowds either captivated by the surface details or ready to dive into what he called "the knowledge of the secrets of the kingdom of God" (Luke 8:10), allowing the deep truths to influence their lives.

In Jesus' day being able to tell a good story was a major skill to have. We might value acting, singing, or whatever else it is that one has to do to be upgraded to celebrity status, but a couple of millennia ago it was the storytellers people would travel for miles on foot to be near. Jesus adopted the communication tools of the day and used them to connect eternal truths with ordinary men and women in simple, accessible ways. Doesn't that sound like the kind of agenda we could be following today? I've got a feeling that if Jesus were around today on the earth, he'd be embracing Facebook, MySpace, Twitter, and anything else he could use to get the good news out to the masses.

Jesus' teaching was a dynamic mix of theory and practice, proclamation and demonstration, all wrapped up in some great God-soaked stories. But in Luke's gospel we don't get to see any of them for the first seven chapters. Matthew and Mark fill their writings with the stories Jesus told, but it looks like Luke is holding something back. Perhaps it's because the story he finally chooses to kick off with is one that is fundamental to everything Jesus stands for. Mark underlines this with Jesus asking his audience, "Don't you understand this parable? How then will you understand any parable?" (Mark 4:13).

So it's clear that every serious follower of Jesus needs to get their head around this story, commonly known as the parable of the sower, even though the sower doesn't really feature all that heavily. In fact it is much more focused on the seed and the soil.

Farming was a massive industry in Jesus' day, so the story would have really struck a chord with his audience. Everyone would know what Jesus was talking about when he said, "A farmer went out to sow his seed …" (Luke 8:5). They would picture the farmer with a large bag of seed on his back, liberally grabbing handfuls and scattering it around him before the plow, which was pulled by a couple of oxen, came along afterward and dug over the ground.

It might be their neighbor they would be picturing, or even themselves. Either way it would have been entirely familiar.

It would have been even easier then than it is today to imagine some of the seed falling on the path only to be eaten up by all the birds that hungrily hovered above the farmer. Some fell on the rock and others among thorns, with the birds able to get at plenty of it. It might have been harder to think of the seed that fell on good soil, producing a crop of a hundred times what was sown. Why? Everyone knew that a bumper crop was something in the region of seven to ten times what was sown. So when Jesus mentioned there being a hundredfold return, it was ridiculously over-the-top. Then, having told this story without any explanation at all, Jesus called out, "He who has ears to hear, let him hear" (verse 8).

How frustrating for the disciples! I'm sure they were thinking, *What on earth has a nice little story about a farmer sowing seed got to do with God's master plan to overthrow Herod and the Romans?* So they tracked Jesus down and asked him to elaborate. Thankfully—for us as well as for them—Jesus' reply was full of things that help us in our own attempts to sow the seed of the kingdom of God.

First, we are meant to scatter the seed of the Word of God as liberally as possible. Our jobs aren't done until every man, woman, and child in our area has had the opportunity to hear the Word of God and see it demonstrated in actions. Every Christian is like a farmer with a great big bag of seed on his back, and it's there for us to sow. I'm convinced that this kingdom stuff isn't going to grow in our cities, towns, and villages unless we put some serious hard work into spreading it around. And we need to make sure we're not staying inside those greenhouses that we like to call church; the seeds need to get scattered out there in the fields, where they are needed most.

Jesus then went on to explain that as we undertake this liberal sowing of the gospel, we can expect to see four kinds of reactions in the hearts of people as they hear about Jesus. The reactions are represented by the four different types of soil. Jesus' story might be two thousand years old, but it still connects with us today. Many of us feel discouraged when we do our very best and it seems that nothing is happening. It's as if you've sown the gospel seed and it's fallen underfoot and been trampled on. And then there are times when, as soon as we've told someone about Jesus, the Devil sees to it that some chaos gets unleashed and the person is back where he started. But that's the way it was for Jesus, and sometimes that's the way it will be for us. Then the only option facing us is yet more praying and more sowing.

We are surrounded by people whose hearts are rock hard and seemingly impenetrable. Even the most powerful gospel preaching and prayer, the most sacrificial kindness, or the miraculous signs appear unable to break through to hearts like these. Jesus understands this, and in Luke 8:6, he explains that the seed can take root in this kind of person but only once he has the right "moisture." If not, then at the first time of testing he'll simply fall away (verse 13).

We see this so often. One of the great sadnesses at The Message is watching rock-hard people fall away from God. Even though they have made genuine commitments at some point, it often happens that once their faith starts to get tested with the trials of life, everything falls apart again. We've seen drug addicts and alcoholics who have come to Jesus wreck their lives again once old family wounds get reopened or old cronies get their claws back in. I wish it wasn't this way, but I don't think we can do anything other than accept it and work harder to set up intensive discipleship programs for new Christians … so that the moisture increases, allowing new seeds to grow.

Not long ago a beautiful thing happened in one of the prisons where we work. A guy I'll call Dean, who comes from one of the most notorious criminal gangs in Manchester, had heard that one of his family members had been murdered. Things were made worse by the fact that he wasn't going to be allowed to go to the funeral because of the possibility that all-out war would kick off at the church. So the prison held its breath and expected Dean—as he had always done before—to smash the place up. Instead, to everyone's surprise, he made his way to the chapel, where our team was holding an Alpha course, along with several guys who had recently been radically converted. Dean listened to their stories and then accepted their invitation to the baptism service that was happening later on in the chapel. The armed robber, the arsonist, and the knife criminal movingly shared their stories at the service as they went down into the water, their bodies getting washed just as their souls had been washed clean by the grace of God. Then they laid hands on one another and started praying that God would bless them in their new lives. To everyone's amazement Dean joined in with the praying. Later on that afternoon, in tears,

Dean prayed for help to forgive the people who had murdered his family member.

After a week Dean looked totally different. He was telling the other guys in the prison just what Jesus had done for him. It gets me every time one of these broken and bad young men come to Jesus. Is there any greater joy than seeing lives caught up in such evil get turned around? Of course it takes more than a moment of repentance to change, and the hard work sets in once the honeymoon period is over. But when lives like Dean's evolve into lifetimes of service, great things happen.

Sadly I can't explain why some of these broken young men fall away, while others power ahead like trains, but that's what Jesus' parable is all about. For our part, we simply have to cooperate with the Holy Spirit in whatever way we can to create the best environment for growth. For us that means putting more time, energy, and finance into helping them find the right church, jobs, training, and homes.

It makes me sad to admit it, but I know that the thorny ground in Jesus' parable applies to more than those who have no faith in God. There are many Christians I know who are caught up in the desire for things that they know are never going to satisfy them. How tragic is that? As they go on their way, they are trapped by what Jesus calls "life's worries, riches and pleasures, and they do not mature" (Luke 8:14).

It doesn't have to be this way. We can change our thorny ground. We can move on and out if we really want to, becoming able to produce fruit and goodness. We don't have to settle for attending church and house group as a religious duty, or going through the motions of singing the songs of full surrender even though we know deep down in our hearts that we love our things more than God and his kingdom. We need to pray hard for those who don't know Jesus; we need to get involved, to take some risks, to shove our hands deep in our own bag of seed and get sowing liberally wherever we go. Even if we don't feel "in the mood" or "right with God" or half as shiny and smiley as the people up on the stage—sometimes getting on and sharing your faith, questions and all, is the perfect antidote to apathy. Yes, some seeds will fall on the path and some will land on the rock and some will end up among the thorns, but it's just as certain that some will fall on good soil. What a joy it will be to see that seed multiply beyond anything we could have planned for.

I thank God that the parable of the soil and seed is not all doom and gloom. It's true that it contains descriptions that should make us all think, but let's not forget that some of the seed fell on good soil, representing the kind of people who have "a noble and good heart, who hear the word, retain it, and by persevering produce a crop" (verse 15). It seems to me that these things have been buried deep in the DNA of people who have made a real impact for Jesus. Take a look throughout history, as well as around you, and you'll see that when someone has a heart for God and a heart for people, combined with the determination to push through hard times and difficult setbacks, great things seem to follow.

At a recent conference our resident worship leader, Andy Smith, went off on one. We were all a little confused when he started playing a song by some weird band named Chumbawamba. The lyrics go something like this: "I get knocked down but I get up again, you're never gonna keep me down." If I'm right, the song is taking a swipe at people who spend their weekends binge drinking, kebab eating, and street fighting their way through our sleepy towns. It was a pretty profound moment for me. I found myself thinking about all the financial challenges that we face as an organization, all the heartache of people falling away, the violence, the vandalism, the personnel issues, and my own inconsistencies. All around me are things that could knock me down and keep me there. But I'm going to get up. I'm going to keep going, to keep dreaming, and to keep believing that, as it says in Galatians, "at the proper time we will reap a harvest if we do not give up" (6:9).

I love the story of what happened when Winston Churchill returned to his old school for prize giving. Being one of the greatest orators of all time, and the prime minister, he was invited to give a speech to the assembled pupils and their parents. It was wartime. The great man made his way to the microphone, paused, and said,

Never give in—never, never, never, never, in nothing great or small, large or petty; never give in—except to convictions of honour and good sense. Never yield to force; never yield to the apparently overwhelming might of the enemy. (Harrow School, 29 October 1941)

And then he sat down. That was it. It may have been one of the shortest speeches of all time, but it helped set the course for an entire nation. You can have all the best strategies and ideas in the world, but if you lack the perseverance and gutsy determination to make them stick, you may as well lie down and stay there.

Perhaps the Lord would want to say to us, "Never, never, never, never give up sowing the glorious life-changing seed of the good news." In fact, can you imagine him disagreeing with it? Of course not. There are hearts out there that are ready to receive the gospel. Often we fail to spot them because we're so busy with our plans or just too fed up with getting knocked down all the time. But there are people out there, just like you and I were once, when we took those first steps toward the open arms of God.

We have to learn the value of perseverance. We have to learn to crave "a noble and good heart." It's no different from when we decide to learn to play the right chords or preach with the right blend of humor and passion. We have to become the sort of people who will stick things out to the end. If we're after a harvest of any size, perseverance is an essential. If we're at all interested in what will happen on the day of reckoning, when we get to meet all the people whose lives have been touched by these small seeds that we've been sowing, then we have to keep on keeping on. Is there really anything more important than that?

HOPE REFLECTED

1. We have all done it—we have all given up at some point. It might have been a relationship, a task, or a dream that we thought at one point God was placing inside us. At some point we decided to stay down on the floor, wearied and worn out by too many knockdowns. Talk to God about your experience, and if you can't remember a time when your perseverance failed you, ask him to bring to mind an example. From there you might need to ask for forgiveness and do something to put it right, or perhaps you need to get rid of the guilt. Pray, and if you can, get someone you trust to help you.

2. Who do you know who's on the floor right now? Think about the people you live and work around, and try to work out if there's someone who just seems to continually get flattened by the struggles of life. How can you help him? Are there practical things you can do to support him? Commit to praying for him regularly and get in the habit of making sacrifices yourself in order to help out.

3. Make time to do a Bible study of all the people who messed up. From Noah's drinking to Samson's wandering eye, Jonah's selfishness to Peter's cowardice, the Bible is full of real examples of real

people. Take a look at them and see what you learn about how God views—and works through—our failings. Are there lessons that you can apply to your own life?

4. Think about the people over whom you've scattered the seed of the gospel. Are there some who seem like thorny ground? How many appear to be little more than rocks, unresponsive to your words and actions? Are you thinking of giving up on them; have you already? Make up your mind to keep on talking to, loving, and praying for them, showing them what the gospel means in as many ways as you can.

7

GOD SAID OKAY AND DISAPPEARED . . .

Luke 8:26–39

At The Message we are devoted to working with young people, in particular the sort that the church has so spectacularly failed to reach. This inability to connect with young people has been going on for generations where I live, and it never takes us long to find yet another example of how desperate the need is around us.

However, while we are sure that this is the right focus for us, we also know that the Lord has said we should never forget the poorest of the poor. As a result we are working in partnership with several key agencies in the developing world. One of these is Compassion, the wonderful child-sponsorship charity that now has transformed the lives of over a million children. Desperate poverty has been changed by the provision of education, health care, food, and spiritual encouragement. We've been banging the drum for our supporters to consider sponsoring children in Haiti, and every time we take on a new member of staff, we sponsor a child. Right now we have around a thousand children who have been sponsored through these efforts.

Recently I had the privilege of traveling to Haiti and seeing many of these children for myself. It was an exhausting experience in every possible way. I sat and prayed at the bedside of a boy living with AIDS who looked like a living skeleton. We visited the island of Gonâve shortly after it had been hit by a hurricane that killed hundreds and left the city all but destroyed. We heard harrowing tales of parents watching their children washed away to their deaths by the mudslide that came down the mountain.

Perhaps the most disturbing experience of all was visiting a women's prison in Pétionville. We were there because my wife, Michele, had read a piece in the *Times* newspaper about the prison. I contacted my friend to ask if he knew anyone who could help while we were out there, and he told me that the director of prisons just happened to be a member of his church. It was the kind of God-coincidence that is so often waiting to be discovered when we manage to get off our own little agenda and look into his.

The inmates are forced to rely on their families for support— families who are also desperately poor. With not enough food and appalling hygiene, up to thirty girls as young as ten are piled into cells and forced to use latrines under their beds. The vast majority of them have never had a trial. We were told that we were the first group who had ever visited the prison to bring gifts and share the good news. The majority of these girls have been raped, some gang-raped. They really are forgotten people.

As I traveled across Haiti, it struck me afresh that Jesus ministered in a similar context. There was political upheaval, abuse of religion, corruption, disease, and despair everywhere. After we had sung, shared, and handed out hygiene packs in the prison, several of the girls committed their lives to Christ. In our minibus on the way back, a friend read out loud these words of Jesus from Luke 4:18–19:

> The Spirit of the Lord is on me, because he has anointed me to preach good news to the poor. He has sent me to proclaim freedom for the prisoners and recovery of sight for the blind, to release the oppressed, to proclaim the year of the Lord's favor.

We all sat there in stunned silence as the impact of these words sank in deeper than before. This was Jesus' calling. And it's our calling too. To bring hope to the most hopeless of situations—both incredibly challenging and the most rewarding thing in the world.

It wasn't all doom and gloom. Haitian Compassion schools really are an oasis in the desert. They are places of great life, health, and opportunity. In fact, as an aside, why don't you do something beautiful today and sponsor a child in Haiti or any of the other desperate countries Compassion works in? Go to www.compassion. com to find out more.

While we were there, we met several amazing men and women who were former Compassion-sponsored children. They told us how without the support they had received they wouldn't have had any hope. Many are now teachers, doctors, and church leaders, including Denil, a young man who pastors a church of six thousand in his spare time. There seem to be hardly any paid church staff in Haiti, and Denil juggles being a leader of Compassion and lecturing at the university along with his pastoral duties. His wife was also a former sponsored child and was in her fifth year at medical school, training to be a doctor. When I asked him what his dream was, he said that one day he would like to be president. He meant it, and none of us could disagree! He did us a little piece for the camera, at the end of which he said, "Haiti for Christ, Christ for Haiti." He meant that, too.

There's a fascinating story in Luke 8. It's Jesus' first miracle in Gentile territory. As ever he's a man on a mission. He has probably heard about this infamous guy who is tormented by multiple demons, who lives among the tombs, and who wanders around naked displaying superhuman strength. So, in typical Jesus style, he doesn't just sit there praying for the poor individual. He steps out of his Galilean comfort zone and makes a move. Jesus gets involved in the world of a man many have previously gone out of their way to avoid.

For Jesus it meant getting in a boat and traveling across Lake Galilee. For us it may mean starting to work on our local tough neighborhood, in the nearest prison or school, or going on a mission with words and actions to the developing world. I don't believe it will take long for any of us to start to feel God close by as he starts to put hurting, broken, hopeless people on our hearts, adding in strategies to bring salvation, healing, and hope to them. Why not try it?

When Jesus and the disciples finally get across the lake, the man they are looking for is waiting for them. Luke 8:27–29 presents a picture of someone made in the image of God with all the potential in the world but in the grip of Satan:

> When Jesus stepped ashore, he was met by a demon-possessed man from the town. For a long time this man had not worn clothes or lived in a house, but had lived in the tombs. When he saw Jesus, he cried out and fell at his feet, shouting at the top of his voice, "What do you want with me, Jesus, Son of the Most High God? I beg you, don't torture me!" For Jesus had commanded the evil spirit to come out of the man. Many times it had seized him, and though he was chained hand and foot and kept under guard, he had broken his chains and had been driven by the demon into solitary places.

Don't you hate what Satan does to people? It may be demonic possession, excessive drinking, drugs, destructive lust, greed, or the love of money that causes so much pain to them and those around them. Satan does this often, and it's all around us. As Jesus' people we are called not just to be angry about it but also to actually get on and do something about it.

So in Luke 8:30, Jesus approaches the man and asks him his name. "Legion" is the answer, and it would have meant something to anyone who heard it. A Roman legion in Jesus' day was made up of six thousand men, so it's clear that the man is letting Jesus know he is stuffed full of demons. Pretty soon those demons start to talk directly to Jesus, begging him not to order them to throw themselves down "into the Abyss" (verse 31). In Jesus' day there was a lot of writing about "the Abyss," and to us it sounds a bit like a horror movie. Back then they believed the Abyss was literally a prison of evil beings, often pictured as a huge lake.

So with his love of all drama Jesus agrees to let the demons transfer into a vast herd of pigs. All those little porkers sprint over to the cliff and plunge themselves over the edge and into the lake below. What's left are the disciples and the townsfolk, chins on the ground in amazement, some of them doubtless a touch annoyed about the fate of their livestock.

But there is one other reaction. The once-possessed man is described beautifully as "sitting at Jesus' feet, dressed and in his right mind" (verse 35). Don't you just love what the good news of Jesus does in even the most broken, messed-up life? It really does work, and it really has lost none of its power.

At this point in many Christian books the author would tell you of his own glorious demon bashing. Sorry, but I just can't. Generally I've been pretty useless when it comes to identifying and then releasing people from demonic possession. I remember on one occasion preaching on this very passage in a big arena. It was such an encouraging evening with lots of young people coming to Christ, but on the way out I heard a ruckus in one of the side rooms. I opened the door to find a skinny little guy from inner-city Manchester being just about held down by six XXL, muscle-pumped bouncers. Over and over again, as if it was coming from some deep, guttural place, this little guy kept on saying the f-word. I knew what was going on, but rather than strike my best ghostbuster pose and command "What is your name?" I froze. I watched as the little guy took on all six of those guys. They laid into one another for a while, until eventually they managed to drag him out into the street, and off he went into the night, still uttering obscenities.

I know I'm a wimp. I knew what I should have done and didn't do it. I was scared and intimidated, and I backed off. I was exactly where Satan wanted me to be. I'm sorry if that, coupled with my stories of nonhealing, makes you want your money back on this book. I just hope that next time I won't bottle it in as much. I'm still convinced that in Jesus' name I have that same authority over the works of Satan and demons. Like so many things in the Christian life, it takes courage and wisdom to get involved.

As I've read this great little story once again, there are four things that stand out for me.

First, Jesus is Lord over everyone, even the most messed up of people. He's constantly planning—in love—to set them free, and Satan knows it. The name of Jesus carries amazing authority, and the gospel of Jesus can set absolutely anyone free. In our prison work what a joy it is to see often deeply disturbed and addicted individuals come to Christ. I'm able to visit various prisons once every few months, and I love it when I see a prisoner who has become a Christian since my last visit. So many times I have to do a double take because he looks so different. And, in truth, he's not really the same person. The hardness, anger, and bitterness have gone, and the loveliness of Jesus is shining through. I'm sure that's exactly what happened on the shores of Lake Galilee.

Second, Satan knows he doesn't have much time left. Revelation 12:12 makes that clear:

> Therefore rejoice, you heavens and you who dwell in them! But woe to the earth and the sea, because the devil has gone down to you! He is filled with fury, because he knows that his time is short.

It won't be long before Satan and all his evil minions are cast into the Abyss forever, and he knows it. We shouldn't be surprised if in the meantime he creates a ruckus.

One of the main ways he does this is through violence. The presence of violence is one of the most obvious signs of his ferocity. Jesus is the Prince of Peace; Satan wants to kill, steal, and destroy. So often, particularly on our inner-city Eden projects, we see violence and vandalism coming in waves. When we see it, we step up prayer in the name of Jesus, and soon enough peace comes back again.

Third, it's gutting to see from this passage how Jesus left. Luke 8:37 is such an upsetting verse. This spectacular miracle is still fresh in the air, with the previously troubled guy before them dressed and in his right mind for the first time in years, and still "the people ... asked Jesus to leave.... So he got into the boat and left." It's amazing how people can resist the overtures of love that God makes toward them. If people see God move, sense his presence, feel his tug on their hearts, but still love their precious things more than him, then eventually God will leave them to it. Those who genuinely reject the cost of commitment will find that the gospel tends to leave them even more bound than before.

Recently Michele and I were away for our silver wedding anniversary in Greece. I was reading the autobiography of Duncan Bannatyne—one of Britain's most successful entrepreneurs. It is a rip-roaring tale of how this ruthless guy goes from owning one ice-cream truck in Glasgow to a huge chain of health clubs, bars, hotels, and much more. Just before we went out to laze on the beach and read our books, we prayed together briefly and went through our Bible notes. The reading went like this:

"For me, to live is Christ." Those words don't
work any other way. Try it: a) For me, to live
is money … to die is to leave it all behind. b)
For me, to live is fame … to die is to be quickly
forgotten. c) For me, to live is power and influence … to die is to be replaced by others. d)
For me, to live is possessions … to die is to
depart empty-handed. Somehow the words
fall flat, don't they? So what's the bottom line?
It's this: The secret of living is the same as the
secret of joy; both revolve around Christ. Don't
try to pursue happiness, just cultivate a Christ-
centered, Christ-controlled life, and you'll have
more happiness than you know what to do
with! (*Anyone Can Do It*, Orion, 2006, p. 231)

We got to the beach and I started reading my book. It suddenly
changed altogether and the chapter in question was retelling
Bannatyne's visit to an orphanage run by Christians in Romania.
It's obvious that he felt a little similar to how we did in Haiti.
Grieved by their poverty but moved by the significant work of the
Christians, he suddenly bares his soul and says this:

For me the tears came at about ten o' clock
that night. I went outside and found a quiet

place at the side of the house. I couldn't stop the tears, my face was wet, my nose began to run and I was a mess. I had no choice but to let the tears flow; and they just kept pouring out of me and wouldn't stop. After many minutes I began to get the feeling that I wasn't alone.

It was there that God said hello.

I felt that I had been consumed by this presence, that something had completely shrouded and taken hold of me. It was unmistakable: I knew who had come and I also knew why. It wasn't a spiritual thing, it was a Christian thing, and I felt I was being told, "You've arrived, join the faith, be a Christian, this is it." It was profound, and I stood there, stunned, considering the offer and thinking about what it would mean. I knew I wanted to keep on building up my businesses and I wanted to keep making money, and I also knew I wanted to carry on doing all the things I wasn't proud of—I knew I was never going to be this totally Christian guy going to church on Sundays.

So I said, "No, I'm not ready."

And God said okay and disappeared.

How desperate is that? He's not unlike the people in the passage who were more concerned about their pigs than their souls. As soon as I got back from holiday, I wrote to Duncan Bannatyne and sent him the notes I'd been reading that day. I tried as sensitively as I could to ask him, "What does it profit a man to gain the whole world but to lose his soul?" I didn't receive a reply.

Finally, despite all this talk about Haiti and Romania in this chapter, I've still got the feeling that mission at home is often better than mission away. The man Jesus had set free from all those demons was understandably keen to join him on the road and begged him to take him along. But, unlike the other disciples, the command for him was, "Return home and tell how much God has done for you" (Luke 8:39). I like the fact that the man then obeyed and according to the passage "went away and told all over town how much Jesus had done for him." It was Jesus who did it, and the man knew exactly where to put the praise.

The truth is that not everyone is called to traveling ministry. Most people are initially called to tell those around them of what Jesus has done. Because one thing is for sure: If you can't win people for Christ in your own school, university, street, or workplace, you ain't gonna do it in the farthest parts of the earth.

This guy didn't need to send out prayer letters and raise support to fulfill his calling. He didn't need a passport or a company car. Everywhere he looked, he could see people who needed to hear how good God had been to him and how he longed for it to be the same for them.

Is he really so different from us?

HOPE REFLECTED

1. Do you know if you have walked away from something that God placed in front of you? It might be a relationship, an opportunity, or a task. If you know you've avoided something that you were meant to face, then do what you need to do to put it right. Ask for God's forgiveness, accept it, and be prepared to do the same with any people involved.

2. If you're one of those people who love talking about your faith, think about those you know who feel less sure of themselves in these situations. Make time to talk to them and listen to what they have to say about why they find it difficult. Can you help them? Explain what it's like for you, pray for them, and keep on encouraging and supporting them.

3. If you're not so sure about "all this evangelism," try to see things differently. Keeping quiet about your faith makes about as much sense as refusing to invite any of your friends or family to your wedding. Talk about it and pray about it, but at the end of the day you're just going to have to break out of your shell and talk about why you believe what you believe. You don't have to convert

anyone or make anyone cry—God handles that sort of thing. You just have to be honest.

4. Do you feel unsure about the value of overseas development? A little dubious about why we should bother to help poor people when converting them would be so much more fun? Widen your eyes and feed your mind by reading the following: Ron Sider's *Rich Christians in an Age of Hunger* and Shane Claiborne's *The Irresistible Revolution.* Or get in touch with charities like Tearfund and Christian Aid; they'll show why Christians should care about poverty overseas, as well as how great the transformation is that follows when they do.

8

HEAVEN TAKES A BREATH

Luke 9:1–9; 10:1–24

I was in the House of Commons at Westminster. Our local member of parliament was hosting a dinner for us. It was a chance for me to share some of our dreams for the future with potential supporters, and I gave it my best shot. So did our MP, Paul Goggins. But neither of us was as impressive, as interesting, or as persuasive as a twenty-two-year-old friend of ours, Natasha.

Natasha told the assembled guests about her life. Something about all the wealth and power that was soaked into the surroundings made her story even more poignant. She grew up in Hattersley, an area on the edge of Manchester. After her mom and dad split up when she was fourteen, Natasha explained how she felt as though she was losing all hope. She more or less dropped out of school and hung around with her friends, smoking weed all day long and never really experiencing anything other than utter boredom. Meanwhile, our Eden Hattersley project was launched, and the Murphys—a great Christian family—moved into the house opposite Natasha. The Murphys started to make friends with the young people in the area—like Natasha.

At first she was skeptical. Lots of them were, and we're used to it. But soon Natasha and the others began to see that this Christian family was for real, that they loved God, loved their neighbors, and longed to see good things happen in the neighborhood. After a while she accepted their invitation to join a girls' cell group. It was here that she heard about Jesus for the first time. Eventually she signed up for a life devoted to following God.

Natasha explained the massive difference taking this step made in her life. She talked about the impact that the loving support of the Eden team had made on her. Her schoolwork, her relationship with her mom, and her sense of self-worth had all been at rock bottom; before long they were completely transformed.

Since leaving school, Natasha has been on our Genetik youth work training program and has joined the latest Eden team as a key volunteer. That's some turnaround, but the best bit came when she spoke so articulately of her own work on the tough neighborhood she has moved into. It was incredible to hear her open up and say how passionate she is about seeing girls just like her set free and given the opportunity to become the best they can.

I've known Natasha for over eight years. I've watched the transformation from messed-up fourteen-year-old to wonderful, sorted youth leader who is influencing loads of others for good. But even though I know her story well, when I heard her share it all at the House of Commons, I felt so proud of her I wanted to jump on the fancy tables and scream, *"Hallelujah!"* at the top of my voice. If Natasha's story was all we had to show from two decades of hard work in Manchester, it would be so worth it.

I've got a feeling that I had a little taste of how Jesus felt when he sent his disciples out on their first ever missions. It's all there in Luke chapters 9 and 10, including the parts where they come back, pumped up with their own stories of impacting others for their Master.

Luke 9 is a turning point for the disciples. After months of seeing Jesus demonstrate this business of preaching good news to the poor, opening the eyes of the blind, and releasing captives, it's now time for the disciples to go out and do it themselves. Jesus sends them out two by two, with his authority and endorsement, and their return is marked by their joy and delight; they've managed to do the things that Jesus had been doing, but on their own. It's their first time of riding a bike, their first book read from cover to cover, their first day at school, all rolled into one and then some. I can imagine Jesus' excitement in verse 10: "When the apostles returned, they reported to Jesus what they had done."

There's almost a collective sigh of relief in heaven. This gospel message that has to be taken on by individuals really is going to work, even through this scruffy lot. Jesus is on a roll, the disciples are on a roll, and that all-important multiplication has started to take place. It's as if from here on out there will be no going back.

That's how it seems until, strangely, everything seems to go pear-shaped.

One by one Jesus' followers decide that they're not all that keen on remaining committed after all. These may have been the very ones who had been reached by his disciples on their first ministry trip, now already starting to backslide. They come with comments to Jesus' face like, "Ah well, I just need to go and bury my father," or, "Let me just pop back home and say my farewells." These are good excuses in their own way, but is there ever a place for excuses in front of Jesus? And think back to Luke 5 where just the words "Follow me" were enough to have the disciples drop everything and head off into the unknown with Jesus.

Now, if even Jesus himself had to face this kind of discouragement—plummeting numbers straight after the high of an amazing fruitful mission—then maybe we shouldn't be too surprised if we experience something similar. The believer who wants to live on the cutting edge of God's purposes should get used to the idea that life will be a roller coaster. The closer you get to that edge, the wilder the ride is.

How does Jesus respond to the gradual exodus of people who once declared their support? He doesn't have himself a pity party and retreat into solitude. No, his reaction is to ramp up the faith and increase the mission. In Luke 10, straight after these events, he pulls together his B team: the seventy-two. These are not his inner circle, not the twelve core disciples he has invested heavily in, but a new crew of people he can release to act as leaders out there on the mission field.

Once again this is a glorious example for us as we send people out. Before he sends out the seventy-two (again two by two), Jesus calls them together for a pre-mission pep talk, and it contains everything we could ever need to know about what makes mission work.

"Ask the Lord of the harvest." That's the first thing (Luke 10:2). Jesus puts prayer first. How can we be so stupid as to ever assume that we can get away with so little prayer in our missions? All the evidence—both in our own experience and as we look throughout the history of Christianity—is that more prayer equals more blessing. The opposite is true as well: Less prayer equals less blessing. When the Bible says, "You don't have because you don't ask" (James 4:2), that means we don't have our villages, towns, and cities for Jesus because we are not spending enough time asking the Lord of the harvest to set them free.

In recent times at The Message we've started to revive the practice of meeting in prayer triplets. Each of us will think of three friends or family members whom we want to come to know Christ. Together we pray for them and commit to sharing the good news with them in words and actions. We hold ourselves accountable to the other two members of our triplet. It's that simple.

About eighteen months ago things were going really well. We'd seen a number of the people we prayed for come to faith, and I said to Andy and Matt, my fellow tripleters, that the next person I wanted to pray for was a particularly difficult one. My niece, Emma, had made it clear on numerous occasions that she had no time for the faith that most of the rest of our family embrace. So together we prayed for Emma that morning.

The following day my mom phoned me, unusually excited. She'd just had an amazing conversation with Emma, who just happened to walk past a church and see an advertisement for their Christmas services. She had gone along and loved it, signing up for an Alpha course. Months later, having completed the course, Emma became a Christian, got filled with the Spirit, and is now one of the most fired-up believers you could meet. She's involved in numerous ministries to the poor and youth in London and has just given up her highly paid job in the fashion industry to go to Bible college and train to be a full-time youth leader. Isn't that wonderful? What a privilege to partner with God and, through prayer, see people like Emma drawn to him.

Every member of The Message team who is in a prayer triplet has a card to remind him why we're doing this. On the back is a scary quote about prayer from a man named Samuel Chadwick:

> The devil laughs at our work, mocks our efforts, pours scorn on all our labors, but trembles when we pray.

That's the truth. It also happens to be the very reason why the first thing Jesus says to his team of seventy-two recruits is, "Ask the Lord."

On my office wall I have a large pair of framed scissors. A friend sent them to me after a talk I gave. Above one blade it says *prayer* and below the other is written *evangelism*. Underneath are the words "Keep on the cutting edge, Andy." Finding that place of sacrificial, committed prayer and gutsy evangelism in words and actions is essential; it's what will see us really cut through in our communities.

The second thing Jesus says is "I am sending you out like lambs among wolves" (Luke 10:3). I'm sure when they heard this they thought it was a slip of the tongue; surely what Jesus meant was that he was sending them out as big, bad, bold wolves who would go out in his name and chase down Satan's little lambs. Surely he couldn't have meant lambs among wolves? Have you seen what wolves do to lambs? But that's exactly what Jesus said, and it's exactly what he meant, for the simple reason that another key to successful mission is going in the opposite spirit to that which characterizes an angry world. We go out as little lambs—as generous, kind, servant-hearted people—to offer his love unconditionally.

It's a strategy that has worked well at the heart of our Eden projects. There we are, in some of Britain's toughest neighborhoods that are notorious for wolflike behavior, being nothing much more than a little team of lambs. With Jesus' name and through his strength our Eden workers have proved time and again that being opposite to the rest of the world brings great results.

The next thing Jesus says to them is also interesting:

> Do not take a purse or bag or sandals; and
> do not greet anyone on the road. When you
> enter a house, first say, "Peace to this house."
> If a man of peace is there, your peace will rest
> on him; if not, it will return to you. Stay in
> that house, eating and drinking whatever they
> give you, for the worker deserves his wages.
> Do not move around from house to house.
> (verses 4–7)

The Lord is letting them know that the mission of God is a faith journey from beginning to end. We need to be utterly dependent on him as we go out. We need to fully expect that he will supply every person and every penny as we do. The impression Jesus gives is of a frantic, faith-filled whirlwind of a tour. How great would it be if that described more of our efforts in his name?

Last of all there's the line in verse 9: "Heal the sick who are there and tell them …" There it is again, word and action, and the expectation that his people will do exactly what he did.

From the moment of my being born again, I have had full access to all I need in order to do this. Moving forward in the Christian life is not so much a question of me getting more of God—but often much more a question of the Spirit getting more of me. And that's where the problems come in; for most of us there is so much resistance to letting God take control.

Pride, fear, and sin can somehow cause what God has put in us to get buried deep inside. Jesus wasn't going to accept that for the seventy-two, and he's not having it for us. He wanted them to preach and to see great salvation; he wanted them to pray for the sick and see great healings, to care for the poor and see the chains of injustice broken. It was nothing less than he wants today.

So off they went on their whirlwind tour, with the Master's words ringing in their ears. And guess what? It worked! I love Luke 10:17 so much: "The seventy-two returned with joy and said, 'Lord, even the demons submit to us in your name.'" But as much as I love that verse, I love Jesus' response to it even more, as he gets about as excited as we ever see him during his entire ministry:

> At that time Jesus, full of joy through the Holy Spirit, said, "I praise you, Father, Lord of heaven and earth, because you have hidden these things from the wise and learned, and revealed them to little children. Yes, Father, for this was your good pleasure." (verse 21)

Remember how back in chapter 1 we looked at Mary's response to the news of her pregnancy and saw the word *agallio,* meaning "to freak out with excitement"? Well, we've got another *agallio* moment here! Jesus is freaking out with joy as the good news goes to a whole new level of multiplication. Don't you love the thought of bringing joy to Jesus like the seventy-two did? How great would it be to have him rejoicing over our attempts to bring his transforming love to a world in need?

We all know it's what Christians must do; we know it's our duty to make Jesus known to a world that is lost without him. But it is also an absolute joy to think of him getting excited about what we do and getting the reward he deserves for his unbelievable sacrifice on the cross.

A few weeks ago I had an *agallio* moment of my own. It was at the Manchester Apollo, a large rock venue in the city center. It's a special place for us because it's where The Message started over twenty years ago when my brother Simon and I booked it—in faith—for a week and encouraged lots of local churches to do creative mission events in the buildup. I've performed and preached on that stage dozens of times since then, but this time I was in the audience alongside around 3,500 screaming school kids. They'd all come along at the end of a month of intensive schoolwork. Three of our Message bands performed, and on stage were plenty of people who themselves had come to faith through our work, as well as several who had been trained and released through our Genetik Training School.

They really did an amazing job, and at the end of the evening the young people were invited to surrender their lives to Jesus. Over four hundred did just that, and to put it mildly, I was excited! To think that over twenty years after it had all started we could still fill venues like that, that we could still present the gospel so relevantly and powerfully ... and that I could sit back and watch it all happen; it did me in. I also knew how messed up some of the performers had been before they met Jesus, and I'd seen how they had gone from being the problem in their communities to being the answer. What a buzz!

Of course, that's what happens when we make introducing people to Jesus the priority that it should be. When those we reach are placed at the center of their own spheres of influence, when they go on and multiply what's grown in them, then the kingdom of God advances. Surely we want to get in on that action, right?

HOPE REFLECTED

1. When you read about prayer triplets, did it make you wonder about starting one up yourself? If so, do it. If not, why not?

2. How's your faith for *agallio* moments? Are you getting enough opportunity to freak out with excitement over the things that God is doing around you? If not, what's the cause? Is it that God doesn't seem to be doing so much or that you're having trouble spotting things? Either way, talk to someone you trust about it. But remember, if you want to be in the kind of place where God's power is close to the surface, you might end up getting involved yourself. Are you up for that?

3. Jesus made it clear to his disciples that faith was vital to the journey of following him. Are you managing to put your faith in the driver's seat, or is it too tempting to climb in there yourself and steer your own course? How would your life look different if you were to relinquish more control of it to God?

4. Prayer and evangelism are a winning combination. Try committing yourself to doing far more of both for the next one, two, or six weeks. You might need to give something up to make room—perhaps cutting down on your TV or Internet time—but make no mistake, you won't regret it.

9

MORE THAN JUST LEFTOVERS

Luke 9:10–17

Make no mistake: Getting down to mission the way Jesus intended is often an exhausting business. It's not a walk in the park, and it's true that we should respond to God's call with the very best that we have.

But it's also important that we don't burn ourselves out in the process. I'm shocked by how many of my friends who lead churches and ministries have had to take time off work because they've burned out. We're not doing anyone any favors if we get to that stage.

So I think that's probably why after the frantic activity of going from town to town on their first mission, Jesus then "took them with him and they withdrew by themselves to a town called Bethsaida" (Luke 9:10). It must have been music to their ears when he suggested they kick back for a while. Isn't it also true for us today; don't we feel better when we slow down, turn off the phone, and concentrate on the love of God? Isn't that one of the best ways to sort out our perspectives and refocus our efforts?

Despite the fact that it was all set up and looking good, however, the break didn't last too long. The next verse tells us that the crowds were close behind them, canceling out any chance of a bit of time off. It's not too hard to guess how the disciples might have reacted, but Jesus' response was to welcome them. He spoke about the kingdom of God and healed those who needed healing. At this point Mark's gospel tells us that Jesus looked at the crowd and had compassion on them "because they were like sheep without a shepherd" (6:34). We need more of that compassion for others, don't we? Can we get it any other way than through Jesus?

The sad truth is that it's not hard to become bitter and cynical toward others, particularly people we hardly know who seem to make demands on our time. Yes, we might want to see them come to faith, but mainly so that they aren't such a pain and so we can get one more notch on our salvationometer. Compassion? Forget about it. Let them carry on wandering around like poor, defenseless sheep without a guide to protect them.

There are some churches we've worked with who have talked about having a "heart for young people." The only problem is that that heart seems to be a little clogged up. Once the kids arrive at their meetings with their skateboards and dogs, reeking of alcohol and behaving in ways that kids with dogs and skateboards and

MORE THAN JUST LEFTOVERS   137

booze generally behave, the friendly welcome suddenly turns cold.

It was his passionate heart for people that drove Jesus on and on and on throughout the day, teaching, healing, and serving until late in the afternoon (Luke 9:12). By then I'm sure the disciples had moved on from feeling frustrated by the initial interruption of the crowds to experiencing extreme hunger, fatigue, and a whole new load of frustration. The clue is in verse 12: "Send the crowd away so they can go to the surrounding villages and countryside and find food and lodging, because we are in a remote place here." Perhaps they thought they were acting heroically, being all concerned about the welfare of the crowds. Yet it's obvious from Jesus' reaction that something else was going on. Just like us, they were backing away from an opportunity for God to do something. Instead they were after the comfortable option. We can be tempted to do that a lot, and whenever we give in, I'm sure that Jesus will say to us exactly what he said to them: "You give them something to eat" (verse 13).

Wherever we look, we can see people who are starving for God's love, his forgiveness, his freedom, and his healing. The Lord wants to say to every one of his followers, "You give them something to eat." He wants us to take a little of the responsibility on board. Of course the disciples looked out at the vast crowd of five thousand men—which was probably more like fifteen thousand people in total—and all they could see was wave after wave of need crashing against the rocks of their own hopelessly inadequate provision. Yet again they were making the mistake that we also make: They were completely unaware of the one who was right next to them, the very man who was able to meet any need, no matter how great.

Jesus gave them clear instructions in Luke 9:14: "Have them sit down in groups of about fifty …" and then give them the little bit you have and see what happens.

As the disciples took a risk and obeyed their Master, something amazing happened. The pita bread and sardines started to multiply before their eyes. Despite being tired and hungry, I'm sure the disciples livened up a bit at this point. Who knows, perhaps they started laughing and cheering as the faster they passed the food around, the faster it multiplied. Right there, right then, was a living, tangible miracle, happening in their very hands. Before long every hungry man, woman, and child was satisfied. Then the Bible tells us (and I love this bit) that there were twelve man-sized baskets left over. Twelve of them, one for each disciple. It's a great story, and it's typical of Jesus: creative, dramatic, meeting real needs, and demonstrating his love in ways that needy people could understand and would never forget.

If we want to help nourish and feed a hungry world, I think there are three things we could learn from this:

God is really into partnership.

God is really into multiplication.

God is really into extravagant excess.

First, *God is really into partnership*. Clearly Jesus could have done this amazing miracle by himself; he didn't need the disciples. At the end of the day he made the universe with a word or two, so it wouldn't be hard for him to whip up some miraculous food for the thousands waiting on his every word. But the way he has decided to do his work is in partnership with his people. He knew that he alone would die and rise again to conquer sin and death once and for all, but he sent his Spirit so that we could "do the stuff" in every corner of the earth. Might as well start practicing, huh?

How many times have we heard the statement that "God has no hands but our hands, no mouth but our mouth, no feet but our feet"? Well, if that's true, isn't it time we took it a bit more seriously? Isn't it about time we started being those hands, mouth, and feet where we live?

Ephesians 3:20 will help us here. It starts off by praising God because he is able to do "immeasurably more than all we ask or imagine." That's our God: bigger and able to do more than all our plans, dreams, and imaginings put together. Then Paul goes on to explain how God will do those wonderful things "according to his power that is at work within us." That really is the power of partnership: God's awesome world-changing power flowing through ordinary, inconsistent people like us.

When I was a brand-new Christian in the late seventies, I was blown away by a long-haired hippy evangelist named Arthur Blessitt. In fact, it was Arthur's book *Turned On to Jesus* that played a major and significant part in my decision to follow Jesus. He used to travel all over the world carrying a huge wooden cross with him. I particularly remember him being asked on TV by a cynical journalist how he managed to fund the work that took him all over the world. Arthur's answer was genius: "I have a very rich Father."

How true is that! Our God has all the resources in the universe, and he actually makes them available to us so that we can fulfill his purposes in partnership with him.

Remember the famous words of Jesus in John 15, where he explains our relationship with him? "I am the vine; you are the branches. If a man remains in me and I in him, he will bear much fruit; apart from me you can do nothing" (verse 5). Isn't that a perfect picture of our partnership with God? He's the vine, and unless we are grafted into him and have his life flowing through us, we are dead and can achieve nothing of worth. Then again, without the branches, there will be no fruit for him in our communities. Partnership is essential.

The second thing that strikes me from the incident of the loaves and fishes is this: *God is really into multiplication.* John's gospel tells us that it was a little boy who gave his packed lunch to the disciples for distribution (6:9). Once they'd heard Jesus tell them to feed the crowds, I'm sure the disciples must have been a little unimpressed with what the kid had in his lunchbox. How on earth was *that* going to feed a crowd that carpeted a mountain? Yet something made them take it to Jesus, and when he told them to pass it out to the people, multiplication began. All our efforts are never going to get the job done until God starts the multiplication process. Now—do you want the good news? He specializes in it.

There have been several times during our work that I've been aware of this miraculous process taking place. When we started the Worldwide Message Tribe (the school's band we formed right at the beginning), I couldn't rap, sing, or dance. But God undoubtedly loved the heart behind it all. Before we knew it, we were selling hundreds of thousands of albums all over the world, and people were being fed spiritually—all through the little band that we set up to do local school gigs.

It was similar in 2000 when we engaged in our first attempt at mass mobilization of young people to do acts of kindness across the city. We didn't really know what we were doing, but it seemed right. We ended up with eleven thousand young people giving their best in Manchester's toughest neighborhoods, and as a result a whole new model of mission was born. Today I'm convinced that there have been literally millions of people who have been blessed as a result.

Most recently we've been behind Hope '08. We've been trying to encourage all God's people to do more, to do it together, and to do it in words and actions right across the United Kingdom. We set ourselves the goal of five hundred groups of churches working together under this united banner, but multiplication kicked in. Before we finished, we had three times as many (1,497 to be precise) regional groups on board, all doing great stuff. They were doing what the church is meant to be doing. To our surprise we also got invited to meet Prince Charles and Prime Minister Gordon Brown to tell them all about it.

I'm also involved in one more thing that might result in some serious God multiplication. It's called The European Church

Planting Network. Recently we gathered in Portugal to share our ambitious plans for church planting and generally get excited about the future. We've seen hundreds of new mission-shaped churches planted, so we were feeling quite proud of ourselves, reckoning that we'd gotten some pretty tasty results coming out of our work. And then we heard our speaker, Victor John from India. He shared his very simple strategy: no buildings, no paid staff, and an expectation that as soon as a church grows over about twelve members, it will multiply. In the face of loads of persecution he has planted around one hundred thousand churches and baptized a million converts. It's called Holy Spirit multiplication, and it's simply the most powerful thing in the world.

The final thing I'd love you to take away from thinking about this great story is this: *God is really into extravagant excess.* Twelve huge baskets were filled with miraculous leftovers collected up by the disciples. God is not stingy; he is massively generous and over the top in his love toward every one of his people, even the ones he knows in the future will betray and deny him. He's just crazy about people and loves to bless them in a big way.

I remember the joy of tickling my son and daughter when they were little. They laughed so much they almost couldn't stand any more, but every time I stopped they came right back. That's a bit how it is with our Father God when he gives us good stuff over and over and over. "Pressed down, shaken together and running over" is how the Bible describes it (Luke 6:38).

Look at his crazy, wild, extravagant world. Look at Jesus' response to the woman who anointed his feet. Look at all you've done wrong and yet how God still clearly loves you. Do you get the picture? God has more than enough love for me. That might not necessarily mean that I get all the finances in the world, but it does mean that I get to share in his utterly extravagant over-the-top generosity toward the poor, the hurting, and the lost.

In Psalm 133, David describes the blessing that comes when we live together in unity. At a time when a sign of blessing was a tiny drop of oil placed gently on the forehead, David's words make it perfectly clear that God is unfailingly generous. His blessing is like "precious oil poured on the head" (literally over the top), "running down on the beard, … down upon the collar of his robes" (verse 2). Sounds a bit much, doesn't it? Yes it does, and that's precisely the way God's heart beats for his world. Over the top, more than enough kingdom stuff—that's how it happens as his people start to make God-sized plans to make him known. As we lock into real partnership with him and allow his Spirit within to kick-start some glorious multiplication, nothing can ever be the same again.

What can you say to that, other than … *Come on!*

HOPE REFLECTED

1. Are you at risk of burning out? Do you know someone who is? If it's you, dismantle the bit of your ego that's started to malfunction by telling you that "to be *this busy* must be good." Then look around and see who else God could be using if you weren't hogging all the action so much.

2. Do you know churches who talk about having a heart for people but in reality aren't that friendly at all? Try to commit to these three things: to pray for them, to find out what you can admire about and learn from them, and to work with them.

3. Get together with a friend and talk about being the hands and feet of God. What do your feet, your hands, and your life tell about God? Are you happy with things as they are, or do they need to change?

10

TRIBUTE BANDS AND BREAD AND WINE

Luke 22:7–20

Our last passage in our journey through Luke's gospel has the power to transform us completely. If we get our heads and hearts around it, nothing will be able to stop us in our attempts to reach those who don't know Jesus.

Okay, so that's a pretty big claim, but then again, what went on when Jesus was nailed to the cross was the single most transformative event in the whole of human history. Why wouldn't we be transformed ourselves if we allowed it to really sink in? How could we ever stay silent once the truth about Jesus got into our lungs?

In this chapter we'll find ourselves joining with the extraordinary missionary C. T. Studd, who blazed a trail of glory in China, India, and Africa at great personal cost. Toward the end of his life he nailed the truth with these simple words:

If Jesus Christ be God and died for me, then
no sacrifice can be too great for me to make.

I wonder if C. T. Studd would mind my borrowing his theme
and tweaking it a little: If Jesus Christ be God and died for me,
then surely no plan to make him known could be described as too
bold.

But before we get into the events of Luke 22, I need to rabbit
on for a few paragraphs about my favorite band, U2. I want you
to know that I am not one of these Johnny-come-lately U2 fans.
I've been following them pretty much since they left Dublin as
teenagers and were playing to crowds of twelve people in dingy pubs,
supporting bands with strange names such as the Virgin Prunes. In
1977, I even got to share the same stage with them—although to be
honest that's stretching the truth a little. I was helping out on the
lights for my brother's band, called the Bill Mason Band, who were
on stage at the Greenbelt Festival just before U2 were due to go
on. When U2 showed up without any instruments, they borrowed
the Bill Mason Band drums. They absolutely tore the place up,
doing tracks from their forthcoming album *October,* which, in my
humble but completely accurate opinion, is just about the best
Christian album ever recorded. It's hardly an understatement to
say that their journey with God over the thirty-two years since then
has been a bit of a roller coaster. But in that time they've made
some amazing music, managed to stay cool, and Bono in particular
has been busy changing the world. The way he's spent so much of

himself haranguing any and every politician, billionaire, or church leader who will listen about the desperate plight of people in sub-Saharan Africa has been nothing short of a God-inspired passion. So, I love him.

Recently I was doing one of my least favorite things in the world. I was shopping. With my wife. For clothes for her. Now, "All Because of You" happens to be one of my favorite U2 tracks, and it started playing over the shop's PA system. Except … it wasn't the original; it was some horrible, thinned-out Muzak version with a tinny drum machine, weedy guitar, and a vocalist who sounded like an *X Factor* or *American Idol* reject. I was appalled. "All Because of You" is an amazingly anthemlike worship track, and they'd managed to turn it into something thin, shallow, and extremely boring.

What's this got to do with Luke 22 and the Passover meal? I think we've done to that passage what the cheesy Muzak company did to U2. Jesus gave us a feast in which he celebrated with great friends and great food and great wine, and we've too often fallen for the temptation to turn it into something thin, vague, and boring. We've ended up with a religious ritual with a cream cracker and a sip of Ribena. The kids are kept away, and altogether it's so diluted from the original that it's hard to see how we let things get this bad.

In Luke 22, as the hour of the cross approached, we see Jesus starting to face up to the enormity and horror of what was just a few hours ahead of him. I believe that every single cell in his body recoiled. Can you imagine Jesus and the disciples walking into Jerusalem past the crosses on the hillside? Maybe there were criminals hanging on them crying out in agony, going into spasms, and hallucinating because of the sheer pain as the soldiers did their worst. After all, the Romans were expert executioners and knew how to make sure the criminals suffered. Before they got on to crucifixion they used to impale people on a stick, literally shoving a spike right through them, leaving them out in the open air to die. The cruelest part was in the skill that impaling people like this required. If they hit one of the major organs on the way through, then the person would often die quickly, and that really wasn't what the Romans wanted. Death, when used as punishment, needed to be slow and agonizingly painful. Crucifixion was the summit.

Mel Gibson's blood fest of a film *The Passion of the Christ* did us all a favor. Better than any other it gave us a truer picture of the physical suffering of Christ. I know there are those who disagree, but I think that understanding a little about the physical suffering Jesus endured is important to us, just as it was important to the Son of God. It was God's great drama, all part of showing us how terrible our sin is and just how far his love was prepared to go. The disciples didn't get it, even though Jesus had made it clear to them that this was exactly how he would die. How could the Messiah end up crucified? Didn't the Scriptures clearly say that "anyone who is hung on a tree is under God's curse" (Deuteronomy 21:23)?

Have you ever really dreaded something? It might have been a diagnosis of a loved one or a difficult meeting. It's a horrible feeling. Do you think Jesus' hands were sweating? Do you think he had that horrible tightness in his chest? We know he had all that and more a few hours later in the garden of Gethsemane. It says his sweat fell like drops of blood as he wrestled in prayer and asked the Father if there was any other way (Luke 22:42–44). This is a condition that has been known to happen to people at the ultimate level of stress; their pores open up and blood comes out. It's as if the body is under such incredible pressure it is literally getting the life squeezed out of it.

That was our Jesus. As he contemplated what he was going to have to go through for us, his body began to break. And it wasn't just the physical agony; what really disturbed Jesus was being abandoned by his heavenly Father. He knew the perfect joy of an uninterrupted relationship with his Father—he had said before that he did nothing unless his Father told him to (John 5:19). He and the Father were one, and you don't get any closer than that. Yet it was all about to be shattered as he was punished for every rotten, evil, disgusting thing mankind had done—and would do—throughout history. No wonder he dreaded the cross. Not that dreading it caused him to sin—he would have had to have been disobedient for that to happen. Even at that time of terrible agony of soul and mind Jesus was able to obey his Father's will completely.

So in the buildup to these horrific events, at this time of massive pressure, what did Jesus do? He turned to his friends. As he faced the cross, he didn't just turn to his Father in prayer; he turned to the guys he'd spent the last three and a half years with. They had proved themselves to be often weak, self-centered, and proud, but they were his friends. Over the next few hours he would need them like never before.

Jesus said in Luke 22:15, "I have eagerly desired to eat this Passover with you before I suffer." How great it is to spend time with friends when we are in real need, and isn't the same true when we get to be a friend to someone in need? I really hope that you are great friends with people who are struggling right now. I hope you're not so wrapped up in your own world, or so driven by your own digital diary or calendar, that you've got no time to be a real friend to those who are finding life harder than it should be.

A hallmark of a church that gets what mission is all about is that it welcomes people—even the ones who are covered in hang-ups and setbacks and weighed down by burdens. If our church is made up of a weird assortment of outsiders and dropouts, then we're probably on the right track. Remember the nickname Jesus was given by the Pharisees—"friend of sinners" (Luke 7:34). They spat it out and meant it as a massive criticism, but wouldn't we all be in trouble if that wasn't the truth? I mean, if Jesus didn't reach out to those who have messed up, what hope would there be for any of us?

One of the problems with many of our churches is that we are pretty good at being friends with the saints but often useless at being friends with sinners. Too often they end up feeling more condemned, closed out, and rejected by our Pharisee spirit. It was never like this with Jesus; people felt loved, understood, and accepted. Yes they were challenged, but there was never any doubt that Jesus was open to all.

Now Jesus turned to his friends Peter and John and encouraged them to "go and make preparations for us to eat the Passover" (Luke 22:8). My feeling is that Peter and John initially wouldn't have been all that impressed by being given this little errand. Preparing the Passover in Jesus' day was considered to be women's work and hard work at that. I once read an interview with a Jewish woman describing her day preparing the Passover meal for her family. She rounded off by saying, "If you didn't collapse with exhaustion when preparing the Passover, you hadn't done your job properly."

I suspect Peter and John would much rather have sat at Jesus' feet and listened to some rich teaching or shared in one of his miracles. Instead it was time to do the menial and hard work of preparing the lamb, bitter herbs, and unleavened bread, getting the wine in, and making sure the room was just right. Little did they realize as they got on with the job that they were doing something incredibly significant that would go down in history. Did they ever imagine that through their simple acts millions would be blessed?

Isn't that so often the way? As we quietly get on with serving anonymously because Jesus has told us to, the efforts are multiplied on into eternity. I'm convinced this is what happens with our own Eden workers in Manchester. They bury themselves in the toughest neighborhoods and around the nation without any fanfare or public praise. They just get on and serve, quietly giving themselves to the least, the lost, and the loneliest. But God sees it all, he uses their sacrifice, and he blesses it and breathes life into their words and actions. One day—the last day of all—we'll finally understand how much has been achieved through such simple acts of service.

What's going on here appears to be the opposite of what happened when Jesus was in Mary and Martha's home a few months earlier. It was then that Jesus gently rebuked Martha for being busy about the home when she could have enjoyed sitting at Jesus' feet like her sister. Here it seems to be the other way around. Sometimes intimacy is needed to get us filled and to transform our thinking. But at other times we need engagement and action. We have to get out there, sacrificially serving communities in the hope of seeing them changed. Getting that balance right in the church is the massive challenge facing every leader.

As I said at the start, we've learned a lot about "servant evangelism" over the last decade. Again and again we've found that getting our hands dirty is vital. Doing the jobs in a community that nobody else wants to do—and doing them free of charge and with smiles on our faces—has a profound effect on people. So often it's this that God uses to unlock their hearts to Jesus. But it works the way it's meant to only when it's backed up by lots of proclamation. In other words, if we want to see the most deprived areas transformed by the good news of Jesus, we need to get our heads around the four Ps: prayer, presence, proclamation, and partnership. And if we want to do big stuff for God, we've got to be faithful with the small things first.

As the events of Jesus' last Passover meal unfolded, something sank in for Peter and John. Thirty times in Revelation John refers to Jesus as the Lamb, and in 1 Peter 1:18–20, Peter writes these beautiful words:

> For you know that it was not with perishable
> things such as silver or gold that you were

redeemed from the empty way of life handed down to you from your forefathers, but with the precious blood of Christ, a lamb without blemish or defect. He was chosen before the creation of the world, but was revealed in these last times for your sake.

As they shared this meal together, and as they pondered it later on, they must have eventually realized that it was not just another special time with Jesus; what was going on was actually massively significant. Jesus really was the ultimate Passover lamb. Because of his blood there was no longer any need for other sacrifices and no longer any need for judgment. The angel of death will pass over our house on the final day, and we will live forever. If, like Peter and John, we believe that, then what are we doing keeping it to ourselves?

John was the youngest at the meal, perhaps only a teenager. He would have been the one who had the privilege of asking Jesus the questions, just like Jewish children still do today. Here was Jesus, the master storyteller, unraveling the amazing tale of Israel's salvation and exodus. Wouldn't you just love to have been there? Good food, close friends, four glasses of wine, and great stories of God-adventures. Don't you think that's a perfect picture of the kingdom to come? Doesn't that sound like the way it will be when we sit down in perfect community at a banquet and share together our stories of living for Jesus and making him known?

It's amazing how much we see Jesus in the Gospels eating and drinking and partying with his friends. It's another thing that wound the Pharisees up. I'm convinced that food and friendship are key things if we want to grow our churches today. I wish more churches would increase their mission budget and then blow a lot of it on great food, wine, and fun for the community—and then watch what happens.

With each cup of wine the story was told, until Jesus got to the third cup, the cup of redemption and salvation. At this point Jesus would have read the required verse, which could hardly have been more poignant: "I will redeem you with an outstretched arm and with mighty acts of judgment" (Exodus 6:6). But then Jesus went off the script that Jews had used for hundreds of years—the script they still use today. This is how Luke records what came next:

> After taking the cup, he gave thanks and said, "Take this and divide it among you. For I tell you I will not drink again of the fruit of the vine until the kingdom of God comes." And he took bread, gave thanks and broke it, and gave it to them, saying, "This is my body given for you; do this in remembrance of me." In the same way, after the supper he took the cup, saying, "This cup is the new covenant in my blood, which is poured out for you." (22:17–20)

It's easy for us to forget that a few hours later this is exactly what he did. His blood was poured out for our redemption and our salvation, and he gave us our own meal. Why? So that throughout history we wouldn't forget that his body was broken horribly, that his beautiful blood was spilled so that we don't need to fear judgment and hell. Instead we can be free and forgiven; we have something to live for today and a glorious future to come.

Our charge, our calling, our greatest opportunity for joy and satisfaction are all found here: to make sure that as many people as possible hear, see, touch, and feel that incredible message for themselves, so that they in turn can become people who are willing to follow Jesus' example and lay down their lives to serve others.

HOPE REFLECTED

I'd like to close this chapter with a prayer that I thought you might want to join in with:

Lord, you are amazing. Thank you for choosing me and appointing me to bear loads of fruit. Thank you for going through the horror of the cross so that I can be free, forgiven, and filled with your love.

Today I commit myself to knowing you better and to making you known wherever I go.

Please show me what that really looks like and help me make my own bold faith-filled plans to share you with a world in desperate need of what only you can bring. Amen.

CLOSING THOUGHTS

If anyone had a roller-coaster life it was the apostle Paul. Looking back, he summed it up like this:

> I consider my life worth nothing to me, if only I may finish the race and complete the task the Lord Jesus has given me—the task of testifying to the gospel of God's grace. (Acts 20:24)

It is equally true for us: We also have a work assigned to us. We were commissioned two thousand years ago with the last words that Jesus left ringing in his followers' ears—"Go into all the world" (Mark 16:15)—and we've been given everything we need to get that job done. God really is with us as we go in his name, right until the "end of the age" (Matthew 28:20).

Unless we are consistently and contagiously obeying him, then no matter how seemingly successful we are, our lives mean nothing. That might not be comfortable or convenient, but it's the truth.

I remember Luis Palau telling me about a conversation he'd had with his mother when he was about twelve years old:

"Mother," he said, "I don't know if I'm called to evangelism."

Her answer was brilliant. "Luis, Jesus called you to evangelism two thousand years ago. The only thing he wants to know is whether you are willing to obey his call."

Clearly not everyone is called to speak to thousands from a stage like Luis Palau, but every follower of Jesus is called to "do the work of an evangelist" (2 Timothy 4:5). And anyway, our great desire ought to be to make Jesus known through words and actions. If it's not, then I would suggest there is something seriously wrong in our Christian lives.

My theory is that every believer, every small group, every congregation, and every mission agency should have a clear strategy. We all need a plan of who we want to reach and how we want to reach them. And if we want these plans to succeed, I believe each of them should include these nine elements:

1. It must be Jesus-centered and Bible-based.

Now this may sound obvious, but make no mistake, in these politically correct days it's surprisingly easy for us to lose the very things that should be at the heart of what we do. Our faith in

Jesus is our engine, and without him we aren't going anywhere. Without the Bible being our inspiration and central to all we do, we descend into a faith mush and lose all our authority.

So first and foremost our job is to talk about, celebrate, gossip about, act out, demonstrate, and live out what the love of Jesus means for people. We've got to do that in our villages, towns, and cities and allow Jesus to do the wonderful things that only he can do. It's not our clever strategies that need to be at the heart of what we do; it's a crazed, passionate, uncompromising love for Jesus.

In a day when everybody knew that "Caesar is lord," Paul boldly proclaimed the gospel of "Jesus is Lord." How we get a hold of that and work it out in our multicultural society will make or break all our mission strategies.

2. It must be birthed in prayer and worship.

Prayer and worship provide the place to discover God's heart for those who don't know him, as well as uncovering the bold plans to do something about it, and even the power to fulfill those plans. Let me put it another way: If you haven't felt as though you just can't stand the fact that Jesus isn't getting the glory he deserves in your community, then I don't think you have ever really worshipped God. Real worship always results in more mission. It always turns up the heat on our passion for reaching the lost.

Amos 5 is one of the scariest passages in the whole of the Old Testament (and that's saying something). We see God's people gather for a great celebration to praise the Lord. They're about to put on a Really Good Worship Service ... when suddenly God speaks:

> I hate, I despise your religious feasts; I cannot stand your assemblies. Even though you bring me burnt offerings and grain offerings, I will not accept them. Though you bring choice fellowship offerings, I will have no regard for them. Away with the noise of your songs! I will not listen to the music of your harps. But let justice roll on like a river, righteousness like a never-failing stream! (verses 21–24)

Does any of that apply to us today? In our world of slick services and well-marketed worship music, could it be that God would want to say two words to us ... "Shut up!"? Stop singing your songs of surrender and start doing something about the desperate injustice that's out there on your doorstep. Stop obsessing about being cool or slick or well known, and start caring about the cries of the oppressed from the far ends of the earth. Stop using my songs to polish your own ego when there are millions who have not heard the good news in a language they can understand.

In my experience there is nothing that unites believers like passionate prayer for those who don't know Jesus. If we get together across streams and denominations with any other focus, we tend to fall out and start arguing. We get all bogged down with what we think about doctrine and practice, whereas real followers of Jesus (from whatever tradition) are all desperate that heaven be populated. It doesn't matter who bags them first, just so long as we're doing our part to see as many people get to heaven as we can.

3. It must include everybody.

Reaching out is not the preserve of the few with an evangelistic calling. There is no such thing as a pastor or worship leader—or for that matter lawyer or doctor, plumber or hospital porter—who is *not* called to evangelism. Paul challenged timid Timothy to be bold on all occasions, "convenient and inconvenient" (2 Timothy 4:2 in the Amplified Bible). Therefore we need to constantly be dreaming dreams and getting active in mission, whatever our gifting, temperament, or natural inclination. There are people just like you out there, and you're the very best person to reach out to them.

4. It must be focused.

A little while ago people started to say that we at The Message were too tunnel-visioned. At first I was a little upset. Since then I've realized it was actually high praise. The only people who really get things done are those who are focused. Think about light; you can spread it out and offer a dim glow to a wide area, or you can focus it into a beam so tight that it can cut through steel. We need God's people to have a laserlike focus on those we want to reach.

To help get this focus right, we need to ask ourselves questions— questions about whether we feel drawn to a geographical area or people group. Are we here for students or kids on street corners? Are we passionate about our town or just our street? There's no definitive correct answer, but we must know for sure what our calling is. If not, how can we hope to use our prayer, presence, proclamation, and partnership to soak every one of these people in the love of Jesus?

And what's our time frame for all this? Are we here for the long haul, for a short-term mission, or something in between? Knowing the answers to these questions will have a profound impact on how we act.

Perhaps sometimes we cast our net too wide. In our attempts to haul in maximum souls for Jesus, we end up missing out on the benefits that would have come from being more focused on an area or people group. This focus will also help leaders decide what kind of church we need to be if we are to reach the people we want to.

Recently I was chatting with an Anglican vicar about the pioneering church-planting group who had—with a good heart but slightly insensitively—planted a new church at the school right next door to one of his churches. I asked him if he was okay with it, and I loved his answer: "I think it's wonderful. My theory is more pubs equals more beer sold, so more churches equals more Jesus." What a fantastic heart, and how right he is! Some pubs specialize in fizzy lager, loud music, and flashing lights, while others go for the real ale, darts, and comfy chairs. The clientele is determined by the atmosphere. If we are clear, and if we focus on the people we want to reach, it will affect the way we do everything.

5. It must be relational.

There is no point having a heart for mission, deciding who we are going to reach out to and how we are going to do it, unless we understand what it means to be relational. People really do need to see our good deeds if they are to praise our Father in heaven (Matthew 5:16), and people simply aren't going to see much if they don't know us at all. It might be better to talk about being "incarnational"—I believe we have to step into people's worlds, to love them, to care for them, and to share in their joys and pains if we are to see a real turnaround in our neighborhood and in our nation.

Two things that have completely transformed the way we do mission are our Eden projects and festivals. With Eden we're breaking out of the old idea of putting on a Tuesday-night youth club, and instead we're drawing in people who are choosing to live long term in the city's roughest areas. The festival model of evangelism is less about gathering together for a good time and more about coming together with thousands of others with the express intention of handing out a great dollop of kindness to people who need it. It seems to kick-start something. I think both these elements—the sacrificial, anonymous serving and the visible and bold generosity—can be used by God to accelerate things in any area we are trying to reach.

6. It must be repeated.

Clearly God can do anything, and people can be transformed on hearing the gospel for the first time … but, in general, people need to hear the truth about Christ seven times before they are ready to receive him. The trouble is that many of us find it too tempting to give up altogether. If all our prayer, kindness, and sensitive words don't seem to be having an impact nice and quick, then we mustn't give up. We can never tell what's really going on inside someone. Bit by bit the Holy Spirit will be softening people, long before they're ready to make the final plunge. In the words of Churchill, we should never surrender.

7. It must be persuasive.

I've said that everyone must do the work of an evangelist, but that doesn't mean that I don't believe in the specific gift of the evangelist. There are people in the church who are specially called and gifted to win people who don't know Jesus. It's a beautiful thing that God has given his church, and we need to use these people wisely. If you know such a person and you are struggling to see your friends and family won for Jesus, try to sit them down with your evangelist friend and watch what God does. I'd also say that we shouldn't be afraid of big events; there has been a move away from big, bold evangelistic events, and that worries me. Yes, go for the low-key kindness, but let's remember that it's not just a case of either/or … it's both.

8. It must be faith filled.

We simply have to take great risks for the great goal of populating heaven. Time and again I've seen that when faith is based on the commands of the Bible, it proves to be irresistible to God. He will put all his resources at our disposal as we obey him and go out into our communities, determined to do what he's told us to do. There's a guy named Peter Brierley who does all sorts of research on the shape of the church. His latest offering is really fascinating. It's all about large churches in the United Kingdom (which is slightly embarrassing in itself, as a "large" church here is one that has over 350 members … in China, Africa, and North and South America, that's considered small). It seems that most of the large churches here are growing even larger and that those that are expanding are increasingly interested in taking their message out to a world in need. However, when it comes to growing your own large church, the key thing above all others seems to be this: believing that you were going to grow a large church. In other words, the churches who *said* they weren't going to grow very much *didn't* grow very much. Those that believed they were going to grow and acted accordingly have grown amazingly.

It's called faith, and it's the most powerful thing in the universe. And finally …

9. It must be excellent.

Whatever we do, whether it's a meal with some of our friends or a huge citywide festival, we need to do things with excellence. I don't tend to like signs around our HQ, but one has popped up that I do like. It says: Excellence Is Our Minimum Standard. That must be our heart as we try to reach out in Jesus' name. Lovely Christians will put up with poor events, shoddy publicity, and shambolic organization; non-Christians will not. I love it when the church shocks the powers that be with an event that confounds their expectations with its excellence. So let's step up, step out, and come up with our own excellent mission strategies.

I do hope you've found this book helpful, and I hope that as a result you are committed more than ever to following Jesus and forming more ambitious plans to make him known through words and actions in this generation. That's really what you've been put on the planet for.

For the last word I think I'll hand over to probably the most hard-core evangelist I've ever met. His name is Reinhard Bonnke. In his book *Evangelism by Fire* (Kingsway, 1989), he wrote these amazing words:

> The Gospel is eternal, but we haven't eternity
> to preach it. One would think we had that
> long when we view the often leisurely opera-
> tions of the church on the Gospel front. We
> have only as long as we live to reach those who

live as long as we live. Today over six billion souls are alive—alive in our present world, not an indefinite future age which needs to be evangelised. It is the last hour.

So let's go for it!

SUPPORTING THE MESSAGE?

Inevitably there is always a need for more people and more pounds (or dollars, euros, Swiss francs …) and more prayer. If you think you could support the work of The Message Trust in any way, please log on to our Web site for more information. If you would love to work with us in Manchester, or if you would like Andy Hawthorne to speak at any of your events or our bands and theatre companies to do their stuff, log on to the Web site or email us at info@message.org.uk.

www.message.org.uk